This publication comes to you through membership in the

NATIONAL COUNCIL FOR THE SOCIAL STUDIES

and has been funded by the

EXXON EDUCATION FOUNDATION

and

PLOUGHSHARES FUND

With the concurrence and cooperation of the National Council for the Social Studies, the author and the publisher have made special arrangements to distribute this publication to all NCSS members. Such distribution does not indicate NCSS endorsement of any specific view or position on nuclear weapons and arms control, but it does reflect the ongoing efforts of NCSS to stimulate analysis, discussion, and debate of the critical issues of our time.

Order Form

National Council for the Social Studies
3501 Newark Street, N.W.
Washington, D.C. 20016

Please send me _____ copies of "Understanding Nuclear Weapons and Arms Control—A Guide to the Issues" by Teena Mayers at the cost of $5.00 per copy including postage.

Enclosed is my check for $_____.

Name _____

School _____

Department _____

Address _____

City _____ State _____ Zip _____

Tel. No. _____

- -

NCSS Membership Application

I would like to be a member of the professional association of Social Studies Educators. Please enroll me and bill me for the type of membership checked below.

Name _____

Address _____

City _____ State _____ Zip _____

☐ Regular Member (Includes *Social Education*, *The Social Studies Professional*, selected NCSS bulletins, Annual Meeting discounts and all other membership benefits.)
Institution: $35.00   Individual: $33.00

☐ Comprehensive Member (Includes ALL NCSS publications, Annual Meeting discounts and all other membership benefits.)
Institution: $45.00   Individual: $43.00

☐ Subscription to *Social Education* (Available only to institutions): $35.00

☐ Charge to my account with ☐ Mastercard ☐ Visa ☐ Purchase order attached

_____

Acct. No.   Interbank No.   Exp. Date

UNDERSTANDING NUCLEAR WEAPONS AND ARMS CONTROL

a guide to the issues

Teena Mayers

Copyright © 1983 by Teena Mayers
Registration No. TX 1-239-436
All rights reserved

First Edition 1983
Arms Control Research

New Edition 1984
Education in World Issues

Library of Congress Cataloging in Publication Data
Includes Bibliography and Index

Mayers, Teena
1. Atomic weapons and disarmament
JX1974.7.M36   1983   327.1/74 19   83-143250

ISBN: 0-9612042-0-6

Contents

Introduction

For years, the arms control issue was regarded as a complex and intimidating subject debated only by the experts. For this reason, the author, Teena Mayers, formerly with the U.S. Arms Control and Disarmament Agency, devised this book as a guide to understanding a complicated topic.

Because the arms control issue is so vital to our national security, this handbook is being published to provide the following:

- a brief history of the nuclear arms race
- the authority to release nuclear weapons
- facts on the basics of arms control
- the current status of negotiations between the United States and the Soviet Union
- tables and diagrams of the U.S. and U.S.S.R. nuclear arsenals
- the effects of nuclear war and civil defense.

It is simple in style, content, and format with facts and information assembled from documents published by the United States Government and other materials in the public domain.

Specialists in arms control and U.S./Soviet affairs have reviewed and approved the text:

Vice Admiral John Marshall Lee, USN (ret.), former Vice Director, NATO Military Staff; Commander, 7th Fleet Amphibious Forces, Western Pacific; and Assistant Director of the U.S. Arms Control and Disarmament Agency.

Major General John Ralph, former Commandant of the Industrial College of the Armed Forces; Executive Secretary to the SALT Delegation in Geneva; and Senior Military Advisor to the U.S. Arms Control and Disarmament Agency.

The Honorable Paul C. Warnke, former Assistant Secretary of Defense for International Security Affairs; and U.S. Chief SALT II Negotiator and Director of the U.S. Arms Control and Disarmament Agency.

In particular, acknowledgment is due to Michael Krepon, former Director of Defense Policy and Program Reviews with the U.S. Arms Control and Disarmament Agency, for his thoughtful and knowledgeable contribution to this book.

Section I

Since the dawn of the nuclear age, debate has raged about the military uses of nuclear weapons and the strategic nuclear policy that the United States should follow.

The strategic superiority that would enable either side to prevail in a nuclear war will not be gained at the bargaining table. There is nothing to indicate that it can be gained in an arms race.

The best that can be hoped for is a stable strategic balance that can be maintained at lower levels and, for this, no administration has found an answer that does not require negotiated arms control.

1945 · 1952 The Truman Years

". . . the atomic bomb is a means of destruction hitherto unknown, against which there can be no adequate military defense, and in the employment of which no single nation can in fact have a monopoly."

Harry S. Truman
November 15, 1945

When President Truman authorized the use of two atomic bombs in 1945 against the Japanese cities of Hiroshima and Nagasaki, the nature of international security was changed drastically and irrevocably.

In the late 1940's, following the conclusion of World War II, the wartime alliance between the United States and the Soviet Union deteriorated. The spoils of war resulted in the Soviet establishment of puppet regimes in Eastern European countries and the creation of East Germany as an additional satellite. Anti-communist sentiments grew in the United States when it became more and more obvious that the Soviet Union constituted a major threat to world stability.

Even though the United States had a monopoly of **atomic bombs** in the years 1945-1949, some officials and scientists argued that atomic weapons should not be considered as merely another type of military weapon, and that measures should be taken to prevent their use ever again. In their view, atomic weapons could not be used for warfare because of their enormous destructive power.

atomic bombs

Others contended that the U.S. technological lead should and could be exploited. During the Truman Administration, these differing views came into sharp conflict over the development of the **hydrogen** or **thermonuclear bomb**, immensely more powerful than the original atomic bomb.

hydrogen or thermonuclear bomb

3

Baruch
Plan

Although President Truman approved the development of the hydrogen bomb, he also sought unsuccessfully to control nuclear weapons. For example, the **Baruch Plan** was proposed to the United Nations in 1946. This plan called for an international agency to ensure that atomic energy would be used solely for peaceful purposes. The Soviets, however, insisted that U.S. nuclear weapons be destroyed before an international control agency was established. The United States insisted that the international agency be established before it would relinquish sole possession of the bomb. The two countries were unable to compromise the two positions.

When the Soviet Union detonated its first atomic weapon in 1949, the international situation worsened. And the beginning of the Korean War in 1950 effectively precluded possibilities of U.S./Soviet agreement on control of atomic weaponry.

Soon thereafter, intelligence reports revealed that the Soviets were actively at work on the development of the hydrogen bomb. President Truman felt that he had no alternative but to take the next major step in the arms race. In 1952, the United States successfully tested a thermonuclear or hydrogen bomb. A year later the Soviet Union matched this feat.

The nuclear race was on . . .

1953 · 1960 The Eisenhower Years

". . . we witness today, in the power of nuclear weapons, a new and deadly dimension to the ancient horror of war. Humanity has now achieved, for the first time in its history, the power to end its history."

Dwight D. Eisenhower
September 19, 1956

During the Eisenhower Administration, a state of political tension and military rivalry between the United States and the Soviet Union, known as the **Cold War**, doomed any hopes of arms control. Proposals and counterproposals were made but failed to bring to fruition any control or limitation of nuclear weapons.

Cold War

Moreover, the Eisenhower Administration relied heavily on nuclear weapons as a substitute for improved conventional forces—soldiers, tanks, and aircraft—which were far more costly.

John Foster Dulles, Eisenhower's Secretary of State, announced a policy of **massive retaliation**—a doctrine whereby the United States might respond with nuclear weapons to any Soviet challenge any place in the world. President Eisenhower's Secretary of Defense, Charles Wilson, referred to this as "more bang for the buck." The vacillation of the Truman Administration between disarmament and a nuclear buildup was soon resolved by Eisenhower's strong stand for **nuclear superiority**.

massive retaliation

nuclear superiority

Despite the huge American lead in nuclear weapons that existed in the 1950's, the doctrine of "massive retaliation" achieved little success. United States superiority did not prevent the Soviets from suppressing the Hungarian Freedom Fighters in the 1956 uprising, nor did it help liberate other captive peoples of Eastern Europe.

5

tactical
nuclear
weapons

During these years, however, thousands of so-called *tactical nuclear weapons*—artillery shells, bombs, and short-range missiles with nuclear warheads—were developed and deployed in Central Europe for use in a ground campaign by land armies. Their purpose was to deter, and if necessary, defend U.S. and NATO forces against a Soviet and Warsaw Pact conventional attack. These "tactical nuclear weapons" were considered essential to give the United States and its NATO allies a meaningful edge against the superior numbers of Soviet conventional forces.

When the Korean War ended early in President Eisenhower's Administration, there were reports that threats by the Administration to use nuclear weapons had played a key part in achieving the armistice. Others believed Joseph Stalin's death in 1953 was the critical turning point.

Notwithstanding his announced policy of "nuclear superiority," Eisenhower made several attempts at arms limitations and even appointed a cabinet-level arms control advisor in 1955.

ICBM

missile
gap

In 1957, the nation was shocked when the Soviets launched the Sputnik satellite—the first to orbit the globe. More ominous was the fact that the Soviets had successfully tested an *intercontinental ballistic missile (ICBM)*. Then came the Gaither Report, a study authorized by President Eisenhower called "Deterrence and Survival in the Nuclear Age," which concluded that the Soviet Union would soon achieve an ICBM force of sufficient numbers to launch a surprise attack against the United States. The fear that the Soviets were developing ICBM superiority was expressed as the *missile gap*.

Under Eisenhower, the United States increased its bomber force and built intercontinental ballistic missiles (ICBMs). By the end of his term, the United States had about 6200 nuclear weapons. The Soviets, who in 1952 had no intercontinental bombers, no submarine-launched missiles, and no intercontinental ballistic missiles, had developed bombers and ICBMs

6

by 1960—but only a fraction of the numbers in the U.S. arsenal.

Although negotiations began in 1958 to ban nuclear testing, when he left office in 1960 Eisenhower was vocally disappointed by the lack of progress in arms control.

The nuclear race continued . . .

1962

". . . the survivors would envy the dead."
Nikita Khrushchev

1961 · 1968 The Kennedy-Johnson Years

". . . A nuclear disaster, spread by winds and waters and fear, could well engulf the great and the small, the rich and the poor, the committed and uncommitted alike. Mankind must put an end to war or war will put an end to mankind."

John F. Kennedy
September 25, 1961

". . . I want to be the President who helped to end hatred among his fellow men and who promoted love among the people of all races and all religions and all parties. I want to be the President who helped to end war among the brothers of this earth."

Lyndon B. Johnson
March 15, 1965

President Kennedy came to office after a 1960 campaign in which he had warned of a "missile gap" whereby the Soviets had achieved or were achieving a significant advantage in strategic nuclear weapons. When the United States started to receive the first pictures from space, it became clear that the real gap favored the United States by a wide margin.

In the beginning of the Kennedy Administration, U.S./Soviet tensions were running high. Kennedy and his defense officials felt that the Eisenhower-Dulles strategy of "massive retaliation" made little sense and did not take account of the rapidly growing Soviet nuclear arsenal. Conventional weapons would also have to play an important role. Kennedy therefore authorized a buildup of both nuclear and conventional forces.

flexible
response
President Kennedy's buildup, however, was based on a different philosophy from Eisenhower's. The overall military doctrine during the Kennedy-Johnson years changed from "massive retaliation" to what became known as *flexible response*. The idea was to acquire the military forces that could deal flexibly with varying levels of Soviet aggression.

Under the direction of Secretary of Defense Robert McNamara, conventional forces were improved as the primary defense against conventional attack. The first-use of nuclear weapons was not ruled out, but any such use would occur only after Western forces had attempted a conventional battlefield defense but were being overwhelmed by Soviet forces. In such event, the President would authorize the use of NATO's tactical battlefield nuclear weapons. Escalation to long-range strategic nuclear attacks on Soviet territory was contemplated only as a last resort to avoid total defeat.

triad
The strategic weapons programs initiated at the start of the Kennedy Administration led to the formation of our present *triad* of strategic nuclear weapons: *intercontinental ballistic missiles (ICBMs), strategic bombers,* and *submarine-launched ballistic missiles (SLBMs).*

Unlike missile silos or bomber bases on land, which could be located and targeted by the Soviets, submarines at sea—the third leg of the triad—were virtually invulnerable. When the first Polaris missile submarine went to sea, the United States was guaranteed a "second strike" capability; i.e., if our ground-based missiles and bombers were destroyed by a Soviet attack, our missile submarines could then respond with a retaliatory strike that would inflict unacceptable damage on the Soviet Union. For this purpose, Secretary McNamara calculated that 1000 land-based missiles and 41 submarines would be more than adequate. Although we have approximately the same number of strategic nuclear delivery vehicles today, the total number of warheads at that time was only a fraction of those in the current United States force.

Strategies other than "flexible response" were also being considered such as **controlled response,** also known as **counterforce**, emphasizing the targeting of Soviet nuclear forces rather than cities, as contemplated by Eisenhower's doctrine of "massive retaliation." But Secretary McNamara concluded that the only realistic strategic nuclear strategy was that of **deterrence by assured retaliatory capability**. Since neither side possessed the means to defend itself against nuclear attack, the best way to deter the adversary was to have the ability to retaliate with unacceptable consequences in the event of an attack. In popular terms this strategy became known as **mutual assured destruction (MAD)**.

controlled response

counterforce

deterrence by assured retaliatory capability

mutual assured destruction (MAD)

When Lyndon Johnson was elected President in 1964, McNamara had established "deterrence" as the central role of U.S. nuclear forces. Under the policy of deterrence, the purpose of nuclear weapons is to prevent a potential adversary from using or threatening to use its nuclear weapons against the United States or its allies.

The most serious confrontation between the United States and the Soviet Union occurred when Soviet leader Khrushchev attempted to place intermediate-range missiles in Cuba. President Kennedy responded by imposing a "quarantine" or blockade of naval ships around Cuba that resulted in the withdrawal of the Soviet nuclear missiles. Some Soviet face-saving was afforded by President Kennedy's decision to dismantle U.S. missiles based in Turkey. Some analysts of the **Cuban Missile Crisis** argue that the successful outcome was due to U.S. strategic nuclear superiority which, in their opinion, had proved that strategic superiority offered important political advantages. Other strategists, including key U.S. participants in the Cuban Missile Crisis, rejected these claims. They felt that U.S. advantage in conventional forces around

Cuban Missile Crisis

Cuba, especially our clear naval superiority, was responsible for the favorable outcome. The parties appear to have recognized that an attempt to resolve the dispute with nuclear weapons would mean unacceptable damage to both countries.

*Limited
Test Ban
Treaty*

The Kennedy-Johnson years saw the first major successes in nuclear arms control. The **Limited Test Ban Treaty (LTBT)**, putting an end to atmospheric tests of nuclear weapons, was completed in 1963. In the

hotline

same year, the Soviet Union and the United States established the **hotline** teletype to enable leaders of both countries to communicate at a time of crisis.

*Outer
Space
Treaty*

In 1967, the **Outer Space Treaty,** banning the deployment of nuclear weapons in outer space, was completed and signed by the United States and the Soviet Union. In 1968, agreement was reached on the

NPT

NonProliferation Treaty (NPT) directed against the acquisition of nuclear weapons by additional countries.

SALT

In the last two years of Lyndon Johnson's presidency, efforts were made to initiate talks on limiting strategic nuclear arms. Both sides agreed privately that the first **Strategic Arms Limitation Talks** (SALT) would begin in the fall of 1968. But on that day in August 1968 when these talks were to be announced, Soviet forces moved into Czechoslovakia to head off the growing unrest in that country. This, followed by the presidential election and a change in administration, delayed the actual start of the talks for a year.

MIRVs

During this time, the deployment of U.S. missiles with a new technological development called **multiple independently-targetable reentry vehicles (MIRVs)**—a single missile carrying multiple warheads which separate in outer space to strike targets hundreds of miles from each other—made control of nuclear weapons more difficult and less effective.

The nuclear race accelerated . . .

1969 · 1976   The Nixon-Ford Years

". . . potential enemies must know that we will
respond to whatever degree is required to protect
our interests. They must also know that they
will only worsen their situation by escalating the
level of violence."

Richard Nixon
February 25, 1971

". . . the weapons we hold today, and those
we plan for the future, give America a mighty
power. But with such power comes a mighty
responsibility. We must never forget the purpose
for which our arsenal is intended. That purpose
is not to terrify the weak, to provoke armed
confrontation, nor lay claim to that which is
not ours . . ."

Gerald Ford
May 10, 1976

Like the Presidents who immediately preceded him,
Richard Nixon campaigned for the U.S. presidency in
1968 on a platform that called for regaining American
nuclear superiority. Early in his administration, however, he became the first president to accept the goal
of "sufficiency." He recognized that it was impossible
to regain a position where the United States would
threaten Soviet destruction without concern about the
consequences to the United States.

Soviet ICBMs had increased from 20 when President
Kennedy took office, to 200 when President Johnson
was elected, to 800 in 1969. No matter how many
additional nuclear missiles the United States might
acquire, the Soviet forces had grown so large that a
nuclear exchange would devastate both countries.

parity

To counter the growing numbers of Soviet ICBMs, the United States responded with MIRVs. This made possible a several-fold increase in the number of warheads that could be aimed at Soviet targets. By the mid-1970's the Soviets also achieved this MIRV technology, resulting in a large increase in the Soviet warhead arsenal. Under these circumstances, President Nixon and his principal international security advisor, Henry Kissinger, recognized that "nuclear superiority" was no longer possible and that a condition of rough **parity** was inevitable.

detente

The rejection of "superiority" as a goal and the acceptance of "parity" made negotiations possible. The Nixon-Kissinger concept of **detente**—a lessening of tensions—was that relations could be improved by involving the Soviets in a pattern of cooperative relationships such as trade and cultural exchanges, as well as arms control. If "detente" could make the Soviets an involved participant in international economic life, it was hoped that Soviet adventurism would be checked. The continuing rivalry and intermittent animosity between the two countries has led some to reject the concept of "detente." This disillusionment probably reflects exaggerated hopes. "Detente" is not, it must be remembered, anything more than a moderation of rivalry. It is not a synonym for friendship.

SALT I

ABM Treaty

Although the Nixon Administration took steps leading to a large strategic buildup, it also took several important arms control initiatives. By May 1972, two agreements were signed. The first severely limited development and deployment of **defensive** anti-ballistic missiles (ABMs)—missiles designed to destroy attacking missiles enroute to their targets. The **ABM Treaty** provided initially that each side could deploy "defensive missile systems" at no more than two sites. A 1974 agreement reduced the permitted number to one site for each country.

By signing the ABM Treaty, both countries recognized that current and future technology could not provide an adequate and effective defense against nuclear attack. Continuing to build ABM systems would only stimulate the acquisition of even more warheads to overwhelm that defense.

The other part of what came to be called SALT I was an **Interim Agreement on Offensive Weapons** that essentially froze the number of launchers of ballistic missiles. Neither the United States nor the Soviet Union could add to its number of ICBM underground silos in existence or under construction. New missile-carrying submarines could be built, but this would require compensating reductions in the number of ICBM silos. Since the Interim Agreement on **offensive** arms limitations was not a treaty requiring approval of two-thirds of the Senate, it was sent to both Houses of Congress as an Executive Agreement to last for five years or until replaced by a longer-term treaty. Both accords—the ABM Treaty and the Interim Agreement—were overwhelmingly approved.

Interim Agreement

Despite difficulties with detente, the SALT talks continued and the Nixon-Ford years witnessed real progress toward conclusion of a SALT II agreement. In these arms control negotiations, both sides were working under the assumption that a strategic nuclear exchange would mean "mutual assured destruction."

There was also real progress in the technology of nuclear weapons. The Soviet Union began to deploy a new generation of land-based missiles, SS-17s, SS-18s, and SS-19s, far superior to their predecessors—the SS-9s and SS-11s—that could threaten U.S. land-based missiles. As a result, in 1974, Secretary of Defense James Schlesinger proposed greater emphasis on **counterforce capability**—whereby American missiles would be developed, deployed, and targeted to carry out "selective strikes" against Soviet military targets. This element of nuclear strategy was previously given secondary importance by Secretary of Defense McNamara during the Kennedy and Johnson Administrations.

counterforce capability

As long as both sides were willing to operate under the principle that nuclear war could be averted if both sides had an assured ability to retaliate, the need

war-fighting strategy

MX

for new offensive weapons would be limited and the strategic balance would remain stable. But this new "counterforce" policy appeared to contemplate the need for a force that could conduct a "selective and sophisicated" nuclear war. Schlesinger conjectured that Soviet capabilities were beginning to fit a nuclear **war-fighting strategy**, and that preservation of deterrence required new U.S. counterforce weapons. Accordingly, he authorized further development of the experimental missile *(MX)* which would have 10 warheads of unparalleled accuracy.

Vladivostok

Shortly after he succeeded Richard Nixon, Gerald Ford met in November of 1974 with General Secretary Leonid Brezhnev in the Soviet port of **Vladivostok**. Important concessions made there were expected to make possible the speedy completion of a SALT II treaty controlling strategic offensive weapons.

Before the Vladivostok meeting, the Soviets pressed for higher numbers of launchers to compensate for the British, French, and Chinese nuclear arsenals targeted against the Soviet Union. In addition, the Soviet negotiators had insisted that the treaty include the U.S. nuclear warheads on aircraft based in Europe and on naval aircraft carriers adjacent to Soviet territory. Because of the complications with our allies that the latter would present, the United States refused to accept these proposals and insisted on deferring these positions for further negotiation after a SALT II agreement had been signed. The U.S. considered the Soviet demand for numerical advantage to be unacceptable, at least on political grounds. The United States also insisted on including the Soviet Backfire bomber, of shorter range than U.S. strategic bombers, but considered capable of reaching some U.S. targets. The Soviets refused to budge, and negotiations on the Backfire were also deferred.

At Vladivostok, Mr. Brezhnev accepted 1) the principle of equal ceilings of strategic weapons launchers; 2) deferral of the issue of American forward-based systems—weapons based on the periphery of the Soviet

Union—and 3) deferral of the issue of the Backfire bomber.

Completion of a SALT II treaty in either 1975 or 1976 was, however, prevented by two factors. The first was the lack of agreement on the treatment of **cruise missiles**—pilotless aircraft capable of incomparable accuracy. The Vladivostok understanding included ceilings on ASBMs—air-to-surface ballistic missiles launched from an airplane and capable of reaching targets thousands of miles away—a system that has never been deployed. But the United States maintained that cruise missiles were not subject to the same ceilings.

cruise missiles

The second factor, and probably the more important, was the American political situation. Before these issues were cleared up, President Ford found himself involved in a close contest with California Governor Ronald Reagan for the 1976 presidential nomination and was concerned that the SALT process would become a political issue. In an important segment of the American public, there was growing resistance to negotiating with the Russians and to the SALT process.

The arms control talks were stalled . . .

1978

  *". . . as for the Soviet Union, it considers that approximate
  equilibrium and parity are enough for defense needs. We do
  not set ourselves the goal of gaining military superiority. We
  also know that this very concept loses its meaning with the
  present enormous stockpiles of nuclear weapons and systems
  for their delivery. . ."*

                                        Leonid I. Brezhnev

1977 · 1980 The Carter Years

". . . the level of nuclear armaments could grow by tens of thousands, and the same situation could well occur with advanced conventional weapons. The temptation to use these weapons, for fear that someone else might do it first, would be almost irresistible."

Jimmy Carter
October 4, 1977

President Jimmy Carter took office with an eloquent call for reduction and eventual elimination of nuclear weapons. He pledged to cut back defense spending on an annual basis by $5-7 billion.

In the last days of the Ford Administration, a U.S. official intelligence-gathering analysis concluded that the aim of the Soviet Union was to gain military superiority over the United States, that its strategic doctrine contemplated that a nuclear war could be fought and won, and that the Soviets were substantially outspending the United States on defense.

Reports from this analysis soon affected the defense debate in the early days of President Carter's term. After initially cutting defense funds, President Carter subsequently raised them more than enough to cover the effects of inflation.

Instead of seeking rapid completion of a SALT II Treaty along the lines that had been negotiated since Vladivostok, President Carter presented the Russians in March of 1977 with what was called a **comprehensive package**. The U.S. proposal called for deep cuts in levels substantially below the Vladivostok ceilings. Specifically, it called for a 50 percent reduction in the Soviets' large land-based missiles, the SS-18s, but no deep cuts in those systems where the United States had the advantage, such as strategic bombers and

comprehensive package

19

submarine missiles with multiple warheads. However, in return, the United States offered to stop development of the MX missile. The Soviet leadership rejected both this "comprehensive package" and a proposed alternative. The alternative was to sign a treaty based on the Vladivostok understanding without agreeing to controls over American cruise missiles or the Soviet Backfire bomber.

SALT II Treaty

After a short delay, however, negotiations recommenced in Geneva in May 1977. Notwithstanding the growing tension and mistrust in superpower relations, the negotiations continued and the **SALT II Treaty** was finally signed in June 1979. SALT II contained many elements of the comprehensive package but not at levels as low as the first Carter proposal and without reductions in the Soviet SS-18 missiles.

Comprehensive Test Ban (CTB)

A series of other arms control initiatives were also undertaken. Most important was the negotiation of a **Comprehensive Test Ban (CTB)** on any further testing of nuclear explosive devices. The British joined the Soviets and Americans in these talks on a CTB.

ratification

Opposition to the SALT II Treaty had been growing in the U.S. Senate for months. The Treaty did not require cuts in operational bombers and submarine MIRVed missiles where the U.S. was superior, but some Senators were concerned because the SALT II agreement did not count Soviet Backfire bombers, allowed only the Soviets to have missiles as large as the SS-18s, and permitted the Soviets to retain a much larger land-based missile force than the United States. **Ratification** of a treaty requires a two-thirds vote of approval in the Senate. To acquire the necessary support, the Carter Administration mounted a concerted campaign. Secretary of Defense Harold Brown announced the decision to go ahead with the large MX missile and its complicated race-track system of deployment and a commitment to a larger defense buildup. A majority of the Senate Foreign Relations Committee recommended ratification of Salt II, but by a narrow margin.

Then, in the summer of 1979, U.S. intelligence photos from a satellite revealed a Soviet military brigade on maneuvers in Cuba. Recalling the Cuban Missile Crisis of 1962, opponents of SALT viewed this with alarm as another act of Soviet provocation. Further investigation revealed that the Soviet brigade of less than 3000 had been in Cuba for years.

In September 1979, Vice President Walter Mondale, on a visit to China, indicated United States willingness to sell the Chinese military-related equipment. At this same time, there were reports that the United States was moving ahead with plans to install nuclear missiles in Europe capable of striking targets in the Soviet Union.

On December 24, 1979, the Soviet Union launched a massive invasion of Afghanistan.

U.S./Soviet relations plummeted to the lowest level since the Stalin era. President Carter ordered that SALT II be placed on "hold" with no further attempt to gain ratification. The United States cut off most of its grain shipments and all of its technology from Soviet trade. Cultural and scientific exchanges were ended. U.S./Soviet relations were placed in deep freeze.

Presidential Directive 59

In the Carter years, opponents of the strategic nuclear policy based on the "mutual assured destruction" doctrine of deterrence continued to exert substantial influence. As a consequence, President Carter authorized changes in U.S. strategy for using nuclear weapons in the event of war. **Presidential Directive 59** set forth a strategy of selective and flexible use of nuclear weapons based on the assumption that the Soviets might start a "limited nuclear war." It called for the United States to be prepared to respond with "selective strikes" against various categories of Soviet military and industrial targets over a protracted period of time.

Critics assailed the new strategy as one based on a theory that a nuclear war could be limited and could be fought by the United States to a successful conclusion. U.S. officials, particularly Secretary of Defense Harold Brown, sought to rationalize the directive (PD 59) as **not** being a departure from the "deterrence" strategy. Instead, they argued, it was to be viewed simply as a precautionary measure—the U.S. must be prepared to deny the Soviets any advantage, whatever level of attack they might elect to conduct. U.S. forces could and should be designed to disabuse them of notions of victory.

Many advocates of arms control found these nuclear war-fighting concepts—such as those represented in PD 59—to be incompatible with arms control as they increased requirements for nuclear forces and increasingly threatened the security of both sides.

Euromissiles   The Carter Administration also authorized, and NATO approved in late 1979, the deployment of two new missiles in Europe that could reach targets in the Soviet Union. These missiles, the **Pershing II** and the ground-launched **cruise missile**, were intended as a response to a Soviet buildup of SS-20 missiles—an intermediate-range missile targeted mostly at Europe. A Western response was regarded as politically imperative. The NATO two-track response included preparation for deployment of 572 Pershing IIs and ground-launched cruise missiles, unless an arms control agreement made such deployments unnecessary. If the negotiations were unsuccessful, ground-launched cruise missiles would be placed in five NATO countries. The Federal Republic of Germany would receive both ground-launched cruise missiles and the Pershing IIs—a ballistic missile which could strike Soviet targets (but probably not Moscow) in six to eight minutes.

The arms control agreements were suspended . . .

1981 · Present The Reagan Years

". . . we must seek agreements which are verifiable, equitable, and militarily significant. Agreements that provide only the appearance of arms control breed dangerous illusions."

Ronald Reagan
May 9, 1982

During his presidential campaign, President Reagan had suggested that arms control might be facilitated by negotiating from a position of strength. He argued that the United States had fallen behind, and therefore the priority task was to build up our strategic nuclear forces to regain *a margin of safety*. He proposed a $180 billion five-year strategic modernization program which would add 7000 new weapons to the U.S. stockpile over ten years. He pledged to deploy the MX missile but cut the planned force back from Carter's original 200 to 100 missiles.

margin of safety

Some Reagan Administration officials talked about the possibility of limited nuclear war. The McNamara doctrine that nuclear forces could serve only as a "deterrent" to nuclear attack was criticized as inaccurate.

The SALT II Treaty remained unratified and the Comprehensive Test Ban negotiations were suspended. The new Administration displayed a lack of urgency about resuming talks with the Soviets on control of nuclear weapons.

However, in response to pressures from Western Europeans who became troubled by official American statements about *limited nuclear war*, discussions with the Soviets about intermediate-range nuclear missiles began in Geneva in November 1981. The Reagan Administration recognized its responsibility to implement NATO's two-track decision to negotiate while

limited nuclear war

23

it prepared deployment of Euromissiles—intermediate-range missiles that would be able to hit Soviet targets from the territory of America's NATO allies.

*INF
talks*

The ***Intermediate Nuclear Forces (INF)*** talks are very complicated negotiations. Several factors in the talks proved to be controversial. For the past two decades, the Soviets have had several hundred intermediate-range land-based missiles, and the United States has had none. The Soviets insisted that British and French nuclear forces be included in determining the theater nuclear balance; the United States contended that only intermediate-range land-based missiles of the two superpowers should be involved in the negotiations. Both sides possessed large numbers of aircraft equipped with nuclear weapons, but there was no agreement in principle about whether and how to count aircraft capable of carrying either nuclear or conventional bombs and missiles. The Soviets also wanted to count and limit sea-based missiles.

*zero-
option*

The Soviet objective in the talks was to block the deployment of the 108 Pershing IIs and 464 cruise missiles in Europe carrying a total of 572 warheads. The Reagan Administration's opening negotiating position was that these missiles would be deployed unless the Soviet Union agreed to eliminate all of its intermediate-range ballistic missiles—the SS-20s with three warheads each, and older SS-4s and SS-5s with single warheads—a total of approximately 600 missiles with about 1200 warheads targeted against Western Europe. This Reagan position became known as the **zero-option**.

Both sides subsequently modified their positions. The U.S.S.R. first proposed withdrawing a substantial number of SS-20s from European Russia, remaining free to redeploy them against China and U.S. bases in South Korea and Japan. Eventually, the Soviet position was clarified to provide for destruction of some SS-20s as well as the remaining SS-4s and SS-5s together with a freeze on SS-20s aimed at Asian targets. The Soviets argued that this would eliminate more warheads than the 572 involved in the planned NATO deployment.

They also contended that this would do no more than balance the intermediate-range missiles directed at the Soviet Union by NATO, including the British and French.

This reduction was not deep enough to satisfy NATO. Although NATO agreed to lower its deployment of Pershing IIs and cruise missiles in return for Soviet SS-20 cuts, this was not satisfactory to the Kremlin which insisted on no new missile deployments by NATO.

By winter of 1983, the talks had reached a deadlock. When those deployments began in December 1983, the U.S.S.R. walked out of the talks.

The Reagan Administration changed the name of SALT to **START**, the Strategic Arms **Reduction** Talks. Negotiations resumed in June 1982 to reduce strategic forces. The Reagan opening proposal called for substantial cuts in ballistic missiles and their warheads, particularly on land-based ICBMs where the Soviets placed three-quarters of their strategic resources. However, the proposal did not require the United States to cancel any of the planned improvements in its strategic weapons systems—the MX missiles, the Trident I and Trident II submarine-launched ballistic missiles, and the B-1 bomber. Moreover, this proposal would have permitted an increase in U.S. deployed warheads due to the placement of several thousand cruise missiles on strategic bombers, submarines, and surface ships. *START Talks*

The initial Soviet proposal at START suggested that reductions be carried out in categories of forces previously established in the SALT II negotiations. However, the Kremlin stated that reductions along these lines were contingent upon a satisfactory solution to the INF talks—in other words, no Pershing II and cruise missile deployments.

The United States then revised its START position in several respects. The previously suggested limitations on specific categories of Soviet missiles were lifted altogether. Then, in 1983, President Reagan agreed to offer the Kremlin a **build-down** proposal, as suggested by a bipartisan group in Congress. In return, these Members of Congress agreed to support the MX missile.

build-down

The "build-down" idea proposed that new weapons could continue to be developed and deployed as long as a greater number of warheads in the existing forces was retired. Separate ratios were proposed for different categories of nuclear weapons: e.g., 2 Mirved ICBM warheads were to be retired for every new one deployed; 3 SLBM warheads retired for every 2 new ones deployed; and one single warhead missile retired for every new one deployed.

The Soviet Union objected to the "build-down" proposal as another means to cut deeply into its land-based missile forces. Like the INF talks, the START negotiations were clearly deadlocked by the winter of 1983.

Both President Reagan and Secretary of Defense Weinberger proclaimed, as did their predecessors, that there can be no winners in a nuclear war. Yet a Defense Department document—Defense Guidance 1984–1988—announced the strategy that "should deterrence fail and strategic war with the Soviet Union occur, the United States must have the forces that can prevail."

President Reagan announced that he would do nothing to undercut or jeopardize the agreements that have been negotiated so long as the Soviet Union does the same. But SALT I has officially expired, and SALT II has not been ratified. However, the Reagan Administration became increasingly concerned over Soviet compliance with these and other agreements. A report expressing these concerns was issued in January 1984.

Each side continues to develop new systems that pose greater threats to the other's forces. Technology continues to outpace the process of arms control. The risk of nuclear war grows graver day by day.

The arms control talks are deadlocked,
the arms race continues . . .

U.S.-U.S.S.R.
Strategic Nuclear Weapons Competition

Presidential Term	TRUMAN 1945 · 1951	EISENHOWER 1952 · 1960	KENNEDY/ JOHNSON 1961 · 1968	NIXON/FORD 1969 · 1976	CARTER 1977 · 1980	REAGAN 1981 · Present
Strategies		massive retaliation	deterrence/ "mutual assured destruction"	deterrence/ "mutual assured destruction" + counterforce	deterrence/ "mutual assured destruction" + counterforce	margin of safety/ war-fighting strategy
Total Defense Budget in first and last year of term in billions of current dollars.	1945 1951 79.5 45.1	1952 1960 57.1 40.3	1961 1968 44.6 75.0	1969 1976 77.8 106.7	1977 1980 118.9 142.2	1981 1984 176.1 273.0

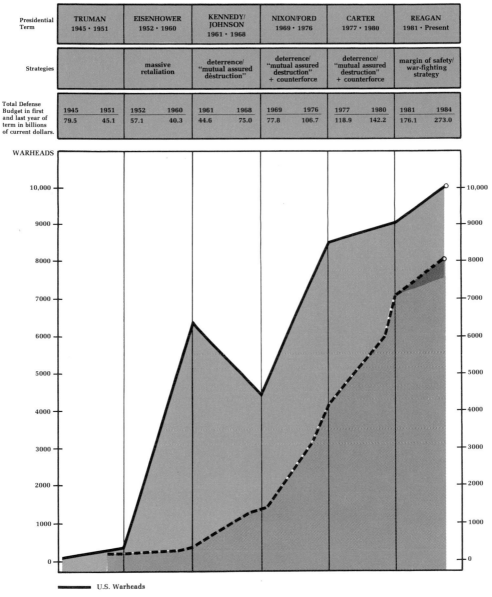

— U.S. Warheads

- - - - U.S.S.R. Warheads

Source: "National Defense Budget Estimates FY 1983,"
Office of the Assistant Secretary of Defense, Comptroller, March 1982

U.S. Administrations

1945 · 1952
President
Harry S. Truman
Secretary of State
James Byrnes
George Marshall
Dean Acheson
Secretary of Defense
James Forrestal
Louis Johnson
George Marshall
Robert Lovett
National Security Advisor
Sidney Souers

1953 · 1960
President
Dwight D. Eisenhower
Secretary of State
John Foster Dulles
Christian Herter
Secretary of Defense
Charles Wilson
Neil McElroy
Thomas Gates
National Security Advisor
James Lay

1961 · 1968
President
John F. Kennedy
Secretary of State
Dean Rusk
Secretary of Defense
Robert McNamara
National Security Advisor
McGeorge Bundy
Lyndon B. Johnson
Secretary of State
Dean Rusk
Secretary of Defense
Robert McNamara
Clark Clifford
National Security Advisor
McGeorge Bundy
Walter Rostow

1969 · 1976
President
Richard Nixon
Secretary of State
William Rogers
Henry Kissinger
Secretary of Defense
Melvin Laird
Elliott Richardson
James Schlesinger
National Security Advisor
Henry Kissinger
Gerald Ford
Secretary of State
Henry Kissinger
Secretary of Defense
James Schlesinger
Donald Rumsfeld
National Security Advisor
Brent Scowcroft

1977 · 1980
President
Jimmy Carter
Secretary of State
Cyrus Vance
Edmund Muskie
Secretary of Defense
Harold Brown
National Security Advisor
Zbigniew Brzezinski

1981 ·
President
Ronald Reagan
Secretary of State
Alexander Haig
George Shultz
Secretary of Defense
Caspar Weinberger
National Security Advisor
Richard Allen
William Clark, Jr.
Robert McFarlane

Soviet Counterpart

1940s · 1953
General Secretary
Josef Stalin
Foreign Minister
Vyacheslav Molotov
Defense Minister
Nikolai Bulganin
Alexander Vasilevskiy

1954 · 1963
General Secretary
Nikita Khrushchev
Foreign Minister
Vyacheslav Molotov
Andrei Gromyko
Defense Minister
Nikolai Bulganin
Georgi Zhukov
Rondion Malinovski

1964 · 1982
General Secretary
Leonid Brezhnev
Foreign Minister
Andrei Gromyko
Defense Minister
Rondion Malinovski
Andrei Grechko
Dimitri Ustinov

1983 · 1984
General Secretary
Yuri Andropov
Foreign Minister
Andrei Gromyko
Defense Minister
Dimitri Ustinov

1984 ·
General Secretary
Konstantin Chernenko
Foreign Minister
Andrei Gromyko
Defense Minister
Dimitri Ustinov

Timeline markers: 1945 · 1950 · 1955 · 1960 · 1965 · 1970 · 1975 · 1980 · 1985

International Concerns

As the United States and the Soviet Union have continued to add to their awesome nuclear stockpiles, the other countries of the world have shown increasing alarm. The multinational **Committee on Disarmament**, which meets regularly in Geneva, has attempted to generate agreements on a "comprehensive ban on nuclear testing" and a "prohibition of chemical weapons."

Representatives of these other countries frequently call the attention of the superpowers to their commitment in the **Treaty on Non-Proliferation of Nuclear Weapons**, signed in 1968, "to achieve at the earliest possible date the cessation of the nuclear arms race and to undertake effective measures in the direction of nuclear disarmament." The danger exists that the effort to prevent the proliferation of nuclear weapons may collapse if the bilateral competition between the U.S. and the U.S.S.R. is not brought under control.

The United Nations has held two special sessions on disarmament in 1978 and 1983, and these have been severe disappointments to supporters of arms control throughout the world.

Although bilateral negotiations between the nuclear superpowers are essential, it is probable that increasing pressure will be applied by other countries to participate in and expedite the arms control process. Impatience with the slow progress of negotiations between the Soviet Union and the United States has led to some calls for unilateral disarmament steps. Some argue that the United States has so many nuclear weapons that it could afford to make reductions even if these are not reciprocated by the Soviet Union. Congressional concern about the strategic balance and popular apprehension about Soviet conduct are likely to prevent any significant unilateral measures from being taken.

It has also been proposed that some type of international agency be established that would supervise the arms control and disarmament process. However, delegating these responsibilities to any outside party or parties seems highly unlikely to be accepted in the U.S. or U.S.S.R.

Slow as the process is and despite the fact that its results have been disappointingly small, there thus far has been no acceptable alternative to the pursuit of arms control through negotiations between the two nuclear superpowers. Three other countries, Great Britain, France, and the People's Republic of China are also nuclear powers, but their forces are dwarfed by the immense nuclear arsenals of the United States and the Soviet Union. Their inclusion in negotiations directed toward setting ceilings and subceilings on overall nuclear weaponry is unlikely until the U.S. and the U.S.S.R. make significant progress toward arms reductions.

On the other hand, Great Britain was a full contributing participant in the now-suspended talks seeking a comprehensive ban on the testing of nuclear explosive devices. The participation of France and the People's Republic of China when the talks resume would lead more nations to adhere to the resulting treaty. Global agreement on a cessation of nuclear testing would greatly enhance the prospects for stability and nonproliferation.

Freeze — At the outset of the SALT negotiations, some U.S. government officials and lawmakers wanted to freeze nuclear weapon developments — particularly MIRVs and ABMs — which were then about to be deployed. They feared that these new weapons systems would dramatically accelerate the nuclear arms competition. Similarly, at the outset of the START talks, many lawmakers and concerned citizens proposed a **mutual and verifiable freeze** on the testing, production, and deployment of nuclear weapons systems. Of primary concern to proponents of the freeze was the continued emphasis of both the U.S. and the Soviet Union on "nuclear war-fighting" systems able to destroy opposing forces.

Supporters of the freeze argued that both sides had more than enough nuclear forces and that the most effective way to stop this spiralling competition would be to halt nuclear weapons testing, production, and deployment that could be verified. Opponents of the freeze believed that suct a halt would be difficult to verify, would lock in existing disparities in nuclear forces, and prevent the U.S. from deploying less vulnerable — thus more stabilizing — nuclear forces.

The U.S. Congress was deeply divided about the wisdom of a comprehensive freeze. After heated debates, the House of Representatives supported the freeze while the Senate did not. In 1984, proponents of the freeze decided to adopt a new approach proposing instead of a comprehensive freeze, moratorium on those aspects of the nuclear arms race that were most disturbing and most amenable to verification of Soviet compliance.

Section II

• **Characteristics of Nuclear Weaponry**

> destructive power
> existing stockpiles
> stable deterrence
> strategic stability
> launch-on-warning
> launch-under-attack

> missiles
> warheads
> reentry vehicles

> tactical nuclear weapons
> intermediate-range nuclear weapons
> strategic nuclear weapons

• **Diagrams**

> Ballistic Missile
> Cruise Missile

> InterContinental Ballistic Missile (ICBM)
> Submarine-Launched Ballistic Missile (SLBM)
> Heavy or Strategic Bombers

• **European Map of Intermediate-Range Nuclear Forces**

• **Comparison of U.S. and U.S.S.R. Intermediate-Range Nuclear Forces**

• **Comparison of U.S. and U.S.S.R. Strategic Nuclear Arsenals**

• **World Map of Nuclear Weapon Countries;**
> **NATO-WARSAW PACT Countries**

• **MX Missile**

• **Defense Systems**

• **Authority to Release Nuclear Weapons**

1862

". . . Someday, science may have the existence of mankind in its power and the human race will commit suicide by blowing up the world."

Henry Adams

1872

". . . It is not probable that war will ever absolutely cease until science discovers some destroying force so simple in its administration, so horrible in its effects, that all art, all gallantry will be at an end, and battles will be massacres which the feelings of mankind will be unable to endure."

W. Winwood Reade

1942

". . . As soon as men decide that all means are permitted to fight an evil, then their good becomes indistinguishable from the evil that they set out to destroy."

Christopher Dawson

1947

". . . If I had known that the Germans would not succeed in constructing the atom bomb, I would never have lifted a finger."

Albert Einstein

Nuclear Weapons

Thirty-seven years after the first nuclear explosion, the control of nuclear arms has become the most essential element in American foreign policy. For the first time in history two nations, the United States and the Soviet Union, have achieved the means to inflict near-instantaneous and catastrophic destruction on each other and the rest of the world. Several other nations have gained the capability to build and acquire nuclear weapons, although on a scale far below that of the superpowers.

destructive power

Some nuclear weapons have greater explosive power than all the bombs dropped in World War II. The two bombs used in the devastation of Hiroshima and Nagasaki each had the explosive force of 13,000 tons of conventional TNT. Today, even the smallest strategic nuclear weapon carries many times the explosive power of the two weapons that destroyed these Japanese cities. We no longer talk of hundreds or thousands of tons, but of megatons—millions of tons.

1 ton	=	2,000 pounds
1 kiloton	=	1,000 tons or 2,000,000 pounds
1 megaton	=	1,000 kilotons or 1,000,000 tons or 2,000,000,000 pounds

existing stockpiles

The United States has a current stockpile of nuclear weapons estimated to have the destructive power of several thousand megatons distributed in approximately 26,000 nuclear warheads of all kinds. The Soviet Union's stockpile of nuclear weapons is believed to be of somewhat smaller size, but with even more megatons. A conservative calculation predicts that 400 megatons would be sufficient to destroy most of an adversary's industrial base and immediately kill hundreds of millions of people.

stable deterrence   Most observers believe a major conflict between the superpowers has been avoided because both have recognized the catastrophic consequences of a nuclear confrontation. Technology today provides each nation with the capability to maintain a sufficiently large, diverse, and survivable strategic nuclear force to dissuade the adversary from nuclear attack. Threatened with catastrophic retaliation, neither power has the incentive to utilize its nuclear arsenal in a crisis situation. This stalemate between the arsenals of destruction is referred to as a situation of **stable deterrence**.

strategic stability   Despite the huge size of the nuclear arsenals, there is no guarantee that the condition of "stable deterrence" will remain in effect. As technology has progressed, nuclear weapons have become increasingly accurate and thus increasingly threatening to the other side. The resulting insecurity has led both sides to continue to arm themselves with still more sophisticated weapons. Increased vulnerabilities have also led to fears of an increased probability that a nuclear exchange could start. Strategic stability is a balance of forces whereby neither side feels threatened and where pressures to arm are decreased. But this condition of **strategic stability** may not survive in the absence of negotiated restrictions on new nuclear weapons.

launch-on-warning   If the nuclear arms race continues uncontrolled, the increased accuracy of nuclear weapons may alter the conditions of stable deterrence. As each side's forces become increasingly vulnerable, the impulse to use weapons rather than risk losing them will become greater, especially at a time of great crisis when there are indications of military preparations on both sides. This is described as a **launch-on-warning** strategy.

launch-under-attack   Almost as grave a risk would be created by a strategy of **launch-under-attack**. This would involve the launch of nuclear weapons on first indication from satellites and other warning systems that the other side's missiles were headed for its targets in the United States or the Soviet Union. This warning could be the result of a computer malfunction. There have been numerous *false alarms* based on computer malfunctions.

With a situation of strategic stability, in which each side is confident of the survivability of its retaliatory forces and comfortable with the military balance, these dangerous doctrines need not be contemplated.

False Alarms—A report prepared by the Senate Armed Services Committee attests to 3703 alarms from January 1979 to June 1980 which were routinely assessed and dismissed; but 147 false alarms were so serious that they required evaluation as to whether they represented a potential attack.

In 1979, an operator mistake at NORAD headquarters inside Cheyenne Mountain in Colorado transmitted and relayed to NORAD fighter bases an erroneous message—*the United States was under nuclear attack*. Ten fighters from three separate bases in the United States and Canada were scrambled and set airborne; U.S. missile and submarine bases across the nation automatically switched to a higher level of alert.

In 1980, a failed 46 cent chip in a minicomputer relayed a similar message, and this time 100 B52 bombers were readied for takeoff as was the President's emergency aircraft. In the Pacific, the airborne command post took off from its base in Hawaii.

Missiles, Warheads, Reentry Vehicles

A *nuclear weapon* is an explosive device that uses the power of the atom. Enormous power is released by either the splitting apart (fission) or fusing together (fusion) of atomic nuclei.

Atomic weapons, created by the United States during the Second World War, were based on the principle of fission. Hydrogen weapons were developed by the United States in 1952 and utilize fusion as well as fission. Both are commonly referred to as nuclear weapons, although most weapons built today are hydrogen weapons.

A *missile* is a vehicle that can deliver an ***explosive device*** (warhead) to a target from distances up to thousands of miles.

The two general types of missiles are:

Ballistic Missile — a missile that is fired into a trajectory or path outside the earth's atmosphere and is then pulled down on its targets under the influence of gravity.

Cruise Missile — a pilotless airplane, about 20 feet long, with wings, a tail, a jet engine, and a computer that acts as a pilot. Cruise missiles fly low adjusting to the terrain, are hard to spot on radar, and are considered to be extremely accurate.

A *warhead* contains the fuse and materials that create the atomic explosion. In the case of a ballistic missile, the warhead is mounted on the front end within the nose cone that constitutes the reentry vehicle.

A *reentry vehicle (RV)* is that portion of the missile that carries and houses the warhead. It is propelled beyond the earth's atmosphere; at the end of its flight, it *reenters* the earth's atmosphere and hits the target.

Some ballistic missiles carry only one reentry vehicle; others carry several, each of which can be directed with high accuracy to widely separated targets. These latter are known as *MIRVs*.

M   Multiple
I   Independently-targetable
R   Reentry
V   Vehicle

Large ballistic missiles can carry ten or more warheads. Currently planned cruise missiles have single warheads only.

The three most commonly recognized categories of nuclear weapons, according to progressively increased ranges, are:

- **TACTICAL or BATTLEFIELD NUCLEAR WEAPONS**
- **INTERMEDIATE RANGE NUCLEAR WEAPONS**
- **STRATEGIC NUCLEAR WEAPONS**

Ballistic Missile

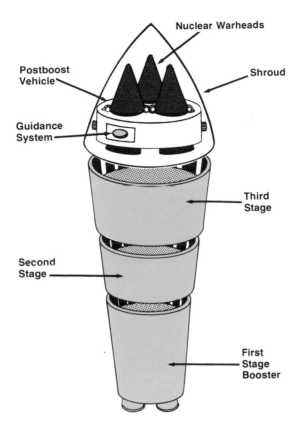

Nuclear Warheads

Postboost Vehicle

Shroud

Guidance System

Third Stage

Second Stage

First Stage Booster

Trajectory (Path)

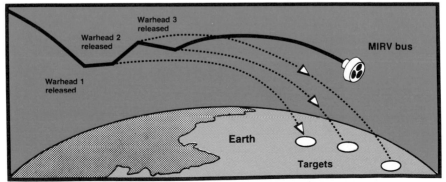

Warhead 3 released

Warhead 2 released

Warhead 1 released

MIRV bus

Earth

Targets

U.S. Department of Defense

Cruise Missile

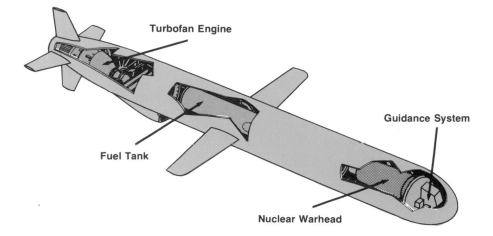

Turbofan Engine

Guidance System

Fuel Tank

Nuclear Warhead

Trajectory (Path)

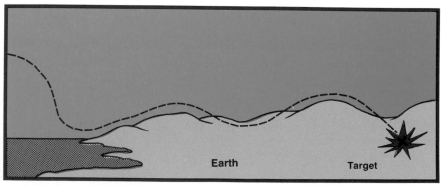

Earth

Target

U.S. Department of Defense

Tactical or ***Battlefield Nuclear Weapons (TACNUCS)***—are short-range, typically 100 miles or less, low-yield (usually well below 100,000 tons of TNT) nuclear weapons designed for combat use on the battlefield. These weapons cannot reach rearguard forces of the opponent or the opponent's homeland.

NATO contemplates use of such weapons to defeat a massive conventional attack by Warsaw Pact forces. Within NATO, however. they remain in the hands of U.S. forces only. Soviet forces are similarly equipped.

Intermediate-Range Nuclear Weapons—also known as Long-Range ***Theater*** Nuclear Weapons—are of longer range, 1000 to 2500 miles, and larger yield than a Tactical or Battlefield Nuclear Weapon, and would be used only in virtually all-out war involving NATO and Warsaw Pact forces.

Intermediate-range nuclear weapons have become increasingly accurate and can be delivered by land-based missiles, submarines and surface ships, as well as by aircraft.

In response to a continuing Soviet buildup in its new Inter-mediate-Range Nuclear Weapons—the SS-20—the NATO Defense Ministries in late 1979 decided to pursue a dual strategy of modernization and arms control. This called for the United States to deploy 108 Pershing II ballistic missiles and 464 ground-launched cruise missiles in Western Europe. At the same time, NATO Ministers expressed the view that an arms control initiative should be undertaken to make the strategic situation between East and West more stable.

Intermediate or Theater Nuclear Forces—those capable of striking the Soviet Union from Europe or vice-versa—are now the subject of complex arms control talks. These INF negotiations started in late 1981. Establishing the terms of negotiation is especially difficult in the European theater because many countries with varying interests and perceptions of the problem are involved.

The planned deployment of the Pershing II ballistic missile in West Germany and the cruise missile in Holland, Belgium, Great Britain, Italy, and West Germany, along with the statements by U.S. officials about possible limited nuclear war, have fueled a strong anti-nuclear movement in Western Europe.

North Sea

Iceland

British SLBMs 64

British Buccaneer Bombers 50

Sweden

Norway

Baltic Sea

Belgium Cruise Missiles 48

Netherland Cruise Missiles 48

West Germany Cruise Missiles 96

Poland

East Germany

Cruise Missiles 160

Great Britain

Czechoslovakia

U.S. F-111 E/F Bombers 161

West Germany

Pershing II 108

Austria

Hungary

French Mirage Bombers 34

France

SSBS S/3 18

Switzerland

Cruise Missiles 112

Yugoslavia

French SLBMs 80

Spain

Italy

Mediterranean Sea

Sicily

Morocco

Algeria

Tunisia

Map of Europe with Current and Proposed Intermediate-Range Nuclear Weapons

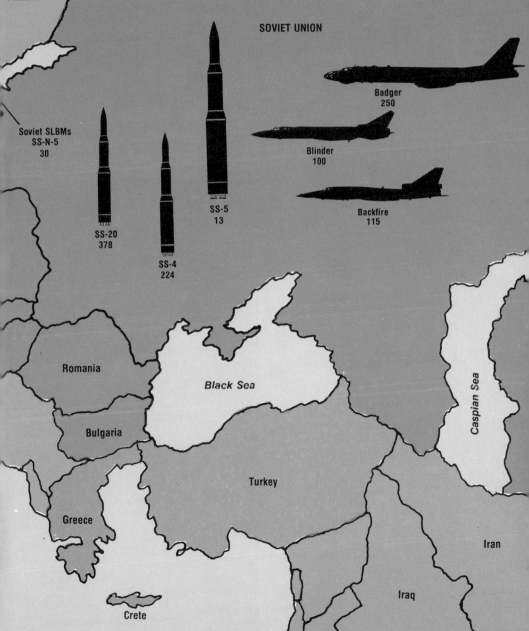

Finland

SOVIET UNION

Soviet SLBMs
SS-N-5
30

SS-20
378

SS-4
224

SS-5
13

Badger
250

Blinder
100

Backfire
115

Romania

Black Sea

Bulgaria

Caspian Sea

Turkey

Greece

Iran

Crete

Iraq

Intermediate Range Theater Nuclear Forces
U.S. and Allied Forces

Weapons	Number	Warheads Bombs	Total Bombs Warheads	Range in Miles	Countries Based-in
IRBM					
SSBS S/3 (French)	18	1	18	2188	France
SRBM					
Pershing 1A (U.S.)	180	1	180	450	W. Germany
Pershing II (U.S.)	9	1	9	1125	W. Germany
SLBM					
Polaris A3 (British)	64	3*	192	2875	G. Britain
MSBS M-20 (French)	80	1	80	1875	France
GLCM					
BGM-109A (U.S.)	32	1	32	1405	G. Britain/Italy
Total Cruise/Ballistic Missiles	383		511		

*Each Polaris A3 has three warheads, but not separately targetable

Weapons	Number	Warheads Bombs	Total Bombs Warheads	Range in Miles	Countries Based-in
Land-Based Aircraft					
F-111 E/F (U.S.)	161	2	322	2938	Britain
Mirage IVA (French)	34	1	34	2000	France
Buccaneer (British)	50	2	100	2063	Britain
F-104 (NATO)	300*	1	300	1500	NATO
F-4 (U.S.)	240*	1	240	1375	NATO
Jaguar (British/French)	80	1	80	1000	Britain/France
Mirage 111E (French)	30	1	30	1500	France
Tornado Bomber (U.S.)	80	1	80	1750	Brit/WGer/Italy
F-16 (U.S.)	168	1	168	2375	Belgium/Neth.
Carrier-Based Aircraft					
A-6E (U.S.)	20	2	40	2000	U.S. Carriers
A-7E (U.S.)	48	2	96	1750	U.S. Carriers
Super Etendard (French)	36	2	72	938	France
Total Air-Delivered Weapons	1247		1562		
NATO Totals	**1630**		**2073**		

*Being replaced by F-16 and Tornado

Warsaw Pact

Weapons	Number	Warheads Bombs	Total Bombs Warheads	Range in Miles
IRBM				
SS-20	378	3	1134	3125
SS-5 Skean	13	1	13	2563
MRBM				
SS-4 Sandal	224	1	224	1250
SRBM				
SS-12/SS-22	100	1	100	563
Total Ballistic Missiles	715		1471	
Aircraft				
TU-16 Badger	250	2	500	3000
TU-22 Blinder	100	2	200	2500
SU-24 (SU-19) Fencer	550	2	1100	2500
MIG27 Flogger D	550	1	550	875
SU-17 Fitter	650	1	650	1125
SU-7 Fitter A	150	1	150	875
MIG21 Fishbed	100	1	100	688
Total Air-Delivered Weapons	2350		3250	
Warsaw Pact Totals	**3065**		**4721**	

Sources: "Military Posture Statement for Fiscal 1985," *Joint Chiefs of Staff*
"The Military Balance 1983–1984," *International Institute for Strategic Studies*

Strategic Nuclear Weapons are weapons that, when launched from either the U.S. or the U.S.S.R., have sufficient range to destroy military, industrial, and urban targets in the other side's homeland.

The three principal strategic weapons systems with sufficient range to reach Soviet and American targets are:

ICBMs - Intercontinental Ballistic Missiles
SLBMs - Submarine-Launched Ballistic Missiles
HEAVY or **STRATEGIC BOMBERS** - Aircraft of inter-
    continental range

These form what is called a ***triad***—the three forces that deter nuclear attack. Both sides are currently creating adjuncts to their triads by developing and deploying advanced cruise missiles that can be land-based or carried by submarines and bombers.

The exact ***strategic balance*** is difficult to measure because both sides have structured their forces in very different ways. Accordingly, a situation of overall parity can be distorted by looking at one possible criterion and ignoring others. Some consider the most important measure of relative strength to be the number of warheads. Others consider megatonnage, the explosive force available on either side, to be the most important criterion of nuclear strength. The United States leads in warheads; the Soviet Union leads in megatonnage.

Since the late 1950's, the United States has opted to build smaller solid-fueled land-based missiles and to place the largest share of its warheads on relatively invulnerable submarines. In addition, the United States has always maintained a large bomber force.

The Soviet Union chose to take a different course. The Soviets have long emphasized land-based missiles. Their missiles are much larger in dimension and in number. In addition, they have built a large number of missile-carrying submarines. The Soviets have chosen not to build a large number of modern intercontinental-range bombers.

Today, most experts agree that the United States leads in long-range bombers, cruise missiles, missile accuracy, and has better submarine-launched ballistic missiles and missile-carrying submarines. These experts also agree that the Soviets lead in the number of land- and sea-based missiles, the lifting power (or throw-weight) of those missiles, the explosive power (megatonnage) of their nuclear weapons, as well as the number of nuclear submarines.

The three strategic nuclear weapons that form the U.S. *triad*, the **Intercontinental Ballistic Missiles (ICBMs)**, the **Submarine-Launched Ballistic Missiles (SLBMs)**, and **Heavy or Strategic Bombers** are defined on the following pages. A chart indicates the number of missiles, warheads, and megatonnage in the arsenals of the United States and the Soviet Union.

I C B M - **I**nter
Continental
Ballistic
Missile

An **ICBM** is a land-based rocket-propelled vehicle capable of inter-continental range in excess of 4000 nautical miles. It is presently stored or housed in a **silo**, a vertical underground launcher. Deployment of ICBMs on mobile launchers is under consideration by both superpowers.

The United States and the Soviet Union arsenals consist of the following ICBMs*:

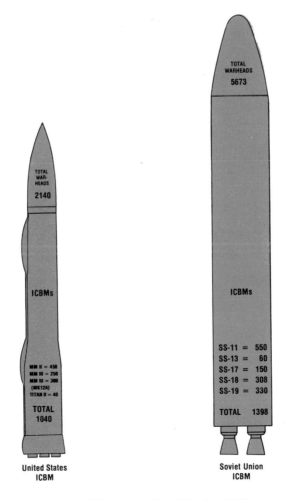

TOTAL
WARHEADS
5673

TOTAL
WAR-
HEADS
2140

ICBMs

ICBMs

MM II = 450
MM III = 250
MM III = 300
(MK12A)
TITAN II = 40

SS-11 = 550
SS-13 = 60
SS-17 = 150
SS-18 = 308
SS-19 = 330

TOTAL
1040

TOTAL 1398

United States
ICBM

Soviet Union
ICBM

*Comparative size is based on Minuteman III and Soviet SS-19

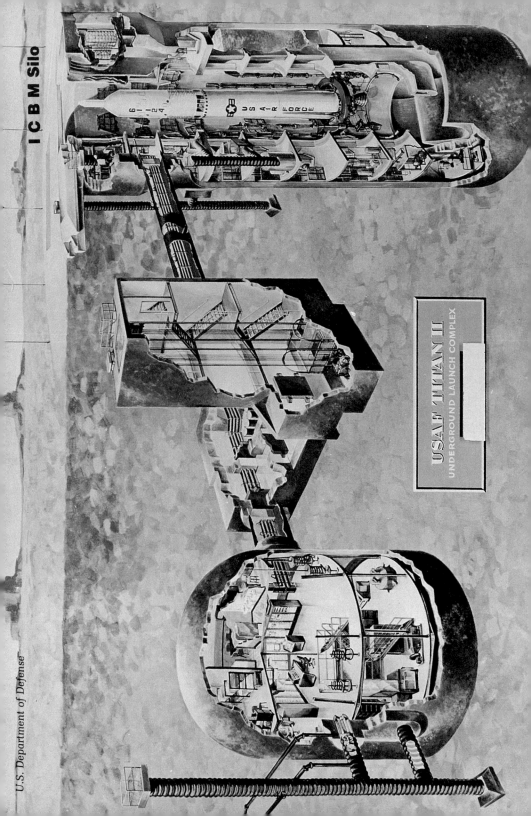

ICBM Silo

U.S. Department of Defense

USAF TITAN II
UNDERGROUND LAUNCH COMPLEX

**I C B M from
Launch Pad**

SLBM

U.S. Department of Defense

S L B M - **S**ubmarine
Launched
Ballistic
Missile

An **SLBM** is a ballistic missile launched from a submarine either sur-faced or submerged. It is stored, or housed, and launched from a **tube**.

The United States and the Soviet Union arsenals consist of the following types of SLBMs*:

TOTAL WARHEADS

1892

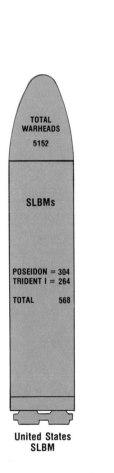

TOTAL WARHEADS

5152

SLBMs

SLBMs

POSEIDON = 304
TRIDENT I = 264

TOTAL   568

SS-N-5   = 30
SS-N-6   = 384
SS-N-8   = 292
SS-N-17 = 12
SS-N-18 = 224
SS-N-20 = 20

TOTAL   962

United States
SLBM

Soviet Union
SLBM

*Comparative size is based on Trident I and Soviet SS-N-18

U.S. Department of Defense

Heavy Bombers

A **Heavy Bomber** is a military aircraft designed to deliver nuclear or non-nuclear weapons against targets on the ground. The HEAVY BOMBER can fly strategic missions at intercontinental distances.

Weapons that can be carried by U.S. Heavy Bombers are:

Nuclear Gravity Bombs—a nuclear device designed to be carried by aircraft and released over its target without independent means of propulsion.

SRAMs - Short-Range Attack Missiles—a guided missile with a range of approximately 75 miles.

ALCMs - Air-Launched Cruise Missiles—a long-range guided missile whose flight path remains within the earth's atmosphere.

ASBMs - Air-to-Surface Ballistic Missiles—a missile which when launched from an airplane would be capable of reaching a target from distances up to thousands of miles. No ASBMs have been developed and deployed.

The United States and the Soviet Union arsenals consist of the following strategic bombers:

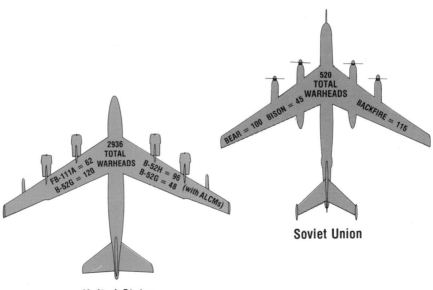

520 TOTAL WARHEADS

BEAR = 100 BISON = 45 BACKFIRE = 115

2936 TOTAL WARHEADS

FB-111A = 62 B-52G = 120 B-52H = 96 B-52G = 48 (with ALCMs)

Soviet Union

United States

51

Total U.S. and U.S.S.R. Strategic Arsenals

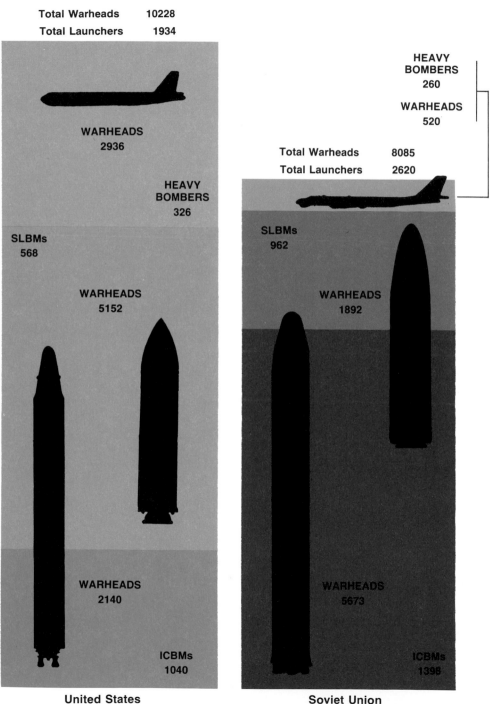

Total Warheads 10228
Total Launchers 1934

WARHEADS
2936

HEAVY
BOMBERS
326

SLBMs
568

WARHEADS
5152

WARHEADS
2140

ICBMs
1040

United States

HEAVY
BOMBERS
260

WARHEADS
520

Total Warheads 8085
Total Launchers 2620

SLBMs
962

WARHEADS
1892

WARHEADS
5673

ICBMs
1398

Soviet Union

52

Total United States Strategic Arsenal

Launcher	Number	Warheads per Weapon	Total Warheads	Yield in MT. per Warhead	Total Megatons
ICBMs					
Minuteman II	450	1	450	1.20	540.0
Minuteman III	250	3	750	.17	127.5
Minuteman III (with MK-12A)	300	3	900	.335	301.5
Titan II	40	1	40	9.00	360.0
Total ICBMs	1040		2140		1329.0
SLBMs					
Poseidon	304	10	3040	.04	121.6
Trident I	264	8	2112	.10	211.2
Total SLBMs	568		5152		332.8
HEAVY or STRATEGIC BOMBERS					
B-52G	120	8	960	1.08*	1036.8
B-52G (with ALCMs)	48	20	960	.20	192.0
B-52H	96	8	768	1.08*	829.4
FB-111A**	62	4	248	1.08*	267.8
Total Bombers	326		2936		2326.0
Grand Total	**1934**		**10228**		**3987.8**

* Average warhead yield (mixed SRAM and gravity bomb loading)
** Not counted as Heavy Bombers in SALT II Treaty

Total Soviet Union Strategic Arsenal

Launcher	Number	Warheads per Weapon	Total Warheads	Yield in MT. per Warhead	Total Megatons
ICBMs					
SS-11	550	1	550	1.00	550
SS-13	60	1	60	.60	36
SS-17 Mod. 1 & 3	130	4	520	.75	390
SS-17 Mod. 2	20	1	20	6.00	120
SS-18 Mod. 1 & 3	23	1	23	20.00	460
SS-18 Mod. 2	115	8	920	.90	828
SS-18 Mod. 4	170	10	1700	.55	935
SS-19 Mod. 1 & 3	310	6	1860	.55	1023
SS-19 Mod. 2	20	1	20	5.00	100
Total ICBMs	1398		5673		4442
SLBMs					
SS-N-5	30	1	30	4.00	120
SS-N-6	384	1	384	.70	269
SS-N-8	292	1	292	.80	234
SS-N-17	12	1	12	.50	6
SS-N-18 Mod. 1	100	3	300	.20	60
SS-N-18 Mod. 2	100	7	700	.45	315
SS-N-18 Mod. 3	24	1	24	.20	5
SS-N-20	20	6-9	150	n.a.	n.a.
Total SLBMs	962		1892		1009
HEAVY or STRATEGIC BOMBERS					
Bear - TU 95	100	2	200	1.00	200
Bison	45	2	90	1.00	90
Backfire TU-22M*	115	2	230	1.00	230
Total Bombers	260		520		520
Grand Total	**2620**		**8085**		**5971**

* Not counted as Heavy Bombers in SALT II Treaty

Sources: "Military Posture Statement for Fiscal 1985"
Joint Chiefs of Staff
"The Military Balance 1983–1984"
International Institute for Strategic Studies

"The Defense Monitor"
Center for Defense Information
"Annual Reports"
U.S. Department of Defense

ARCTIC OCEAN

ARC

GREENLAND

ICELAND

NORWA

EAST
GERMANY

ALASKA

NETHERLANDS
WEST
GERMANY

CANADA

GREAT
BRITAIN

DENMARK

IRELAND

BELGIUM
LUXEMBOURG
²FRANCE
SWITZERLAND
AUSTRIA

UNITED STATES

PORTUGAL

SPAIN

ATLANTIC OCEAN

MOROCCO

ALGERIA

MEXICO

CUBA

VENEZUELA

PACIFIC OCEAN

COLOMBIA

NATO¹ Countries

Warsaw Pact
Countries

BRAZIL

PERU

Countries with
Nuclear Weapons

Countries
interested in
Nuclear Weapons

Countries with
Nuclear Weapons
Capability

CHILE

ARGENTINA

¹North Atlantic Treaty Organization

²France is a member of NATO but its
military forces are not under NATO
command.

World Map of: Nuclear Weapons Countries
NATO and Warsaw Pact Countries

MX Missile
(Missile eXperimental)

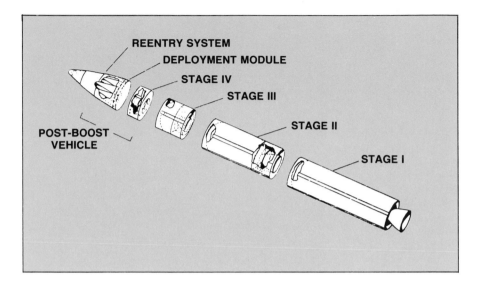

REENTRY SYSTEM
DEPLOYMENT MODULE
STAGE IV
STAGE III
STAGE II
POST-BOOST VEHICLE
STAGE I

The first three stages of the MX use solid propellant and thrust the missile into intercontinental range.

The fourth stage, the post-boost vehicle, uses liquid fuel and contains the new and more precise computers, guidance electronics, and communications equipment that control the missile. It is also designed to carry up to 12 independently targetable nuclear reentry vehicles, but current adherence to SALT II provisions will limit testing and deployment of 10 MIRVs.

U.S. Department of Defense

The MX Missile
(Missile eXperimental)

Intercontinental Ballistic Missiles (ICBMs) comprise the land-based leg of the U.S. triad. The newest American ICBM is the **MX** missile which stands for ***Missile eXperimental***. It is planned to carry ten nuclear warheads. Each warhead can reach a different target; the destination of each warhead can be changed by adjusting the program that the missile is to follow.

The missile itself is 70 feet long, 92 inches in diameter, and weighs approximately 192,000 pounds. Unlike land-based missiles currently in the U.S. inventory, the MX is more accurate, carries more warheads, and has a greater range and targeting flexibility.

The Soviet Union already has ICBMs larger than the MX; namely, the SS-18. Because of the size and accuracy of these Soviet missiles, many have argued that the United States must match these Soviet capabilities. Others have rejected this idea as placing a "hair trigger" on nuclear war. With each side's forces becoming increasingly accurate and therefore vulnerable to a first strike, they fear that nuclear weapons might be used early in a crisis situation to prevent their being destroyed on the ground. Many experts therefore believe the United States should move more of its forces to more secure basing methods.

Planning and development of MX have been underway for a decade, but continuing controversy over the best way to base the missile has repeatedly stalled the program.

In 1972, the Strategic Air Command first proposed an advanced ICBM program to replace the Minuteman missiles deployed during the Eisenhower and Kennedy Administrations. It has, however, proved difficult to find a basing mode that would eliminate the theoretical vulnerability of the U.S. land-based missile force. Since 1972, thirty-four different basing options have been considered. Deep trenches, railroad tracks, and underwater systems are among the many basing modes considered and rejected by several administrations.

In 1979, President Carter announced a decision to go ahead with the MX missile and a complicated ***shell game*** method—a multiple-basing ***race-track*** system of deployment. Two hundred missiles would have moved among 4600 shelters in an effort to confuse Soviet military planners.

President Reagan rejected this approach as being too costly while still being vulnerable to a Soviet attack. In November of 1982, he announced his intention to base the MX in a configuration known as **Dense Pack**. Located in Wyoming, the Dense Pack field would be a 14-mile long rectangle housing 100 MX missiles spaced 1800 feet apart in silos hardened against nuclear effects.

In theory, most of the missiles would survive because the Soviets could not time an attack so precisely as to strike all 100 MX silos at the same time. In other words, the combined effects of the blast waves, radiation, and airborne debris caused by the explosion of the first arriving warheads would destroy the latecomers, in what is called a **fratricide** effect.

Congress was unwilling to support this basing plan as it appeared less survivable than the race-track proposal by President Carter. As a result of this impasse, President Reagan appointed a blue-ribbon panel headed by General Brent Scowcroft to review MX basing alternatives and other strategic issues.

The Scowcroft Commission finally concluded that 100 MX missiles should be based in the existing Minuteman silos. It also concluded that the threat to U.S. strategic forces by Soviet land-based missiles had been exaggerated. While it was true that the U.S. and Soviet land-based missiles might be vulnerable, U.S. bombers and sea-based missiles remained superior to their Soviet counterparts, and both these legs of the triad could deliver devastating blows in the event of a Soviet attack.

The Scowcroft Commission also recommended that the United States proceed to develop a new single-warhead missile which would not pose as much of a threat nor be as attractive a target as the MX. Finally, the Scowcroft Commission advocated changes in the Reagan Administration's negotiating proposals to emphasize the need for a stable balance of forces.

Source: *U.S. Department of Defense*

Defense Systems

"... It is vain to look for a defense against lightning."
Maxum 835
Pubilius Syrus, 1 B.C.

Certain nuclear weapons systems are intended for defensive purposes only. Because of their short range and other capabilities, these weapons **cannot** be used to initiate an attack or to retaliate against Soviet targets.

To provide some measure of defense against a nuclear attack, the United States has developed various **defense systems** such as:

- **interceptor aircraft**, equipped with nuclear as well as non-nuclear missiles, to be used to intercept attacking bombers.

- **surface-to-air missiles (SAM)**, equipped with nuclear and non-nuclear explosives, launched from land and from surface ships against attacking bombers and cruise missiles.

- **anti-submarine warfare forces (ASW)** composed of ships, aircraft, and submarines to be used to detect, identify, track, and destroy hostile missile-carrying submarines.

- **anti-ballistic missiles (ABM)** to destroy incoming offensive missiles.

Much effort and cost have gone into the development of these weapon systems, but the prevailing view among experts has been that they would not work effectively against a Soviet nuclear attack. Incoming ballistic missiles travel at extremely high speeds and are extraordinarily difficult to intercept. Submarines are very difficult to find and to destroy before they launch their missiles. Cruise missiles are extremely difficult to track and shoot down.

Because none of the defense weapons are now capable of preventing the devastation which would be the inevitable result of a nuclear attack, and because no existing technology is adequate to protect against hundreds of missiles carrying thousands of warheads, President Nixon and General Secretary Brezhnev signed the **ABM Treaty** on May 26, 1972 which limited both nations to two ABM sites with no more than 100 missiles each. Subsequently, both sides agreed to reduce the permitted ABM sites to one each. The Treaty was ratified by both countries, is of unlimited duration, and each nation has abided by its terms.

Although new ABMs are forbidden to be deployed, research and development programs have continued, and thousands of interceptor aircraft and radar systems have been built. Yet authorities on strategic weaponry are confident that an adversary's bombers and missiles can penetrate any existing or foreseeable defense system. It is impossible with existing technology to build strategic defensive systems capable of keeping casualties to acceptable levels in event of attack.

However, President Reagan has expressed the hope that new highly advanced technologies will be able to defend against an attack by nuclear weapons. In 1983, President Reagan endorsed a major research and development effort to solve the varied problems associated with an ABM defense. If successful, this effort would require the abrogation of the ABM Treaty.

Many critics believe that the prospect of success is highly unlikely and its pursuit extremely costly. Moreover, if successful, they contend that new space-based weapons could be readily countered by relatively cheap devices like "space-mines" which can orbit next to defensive systems.

Source: *U.S. Arms Control and Disarmament Agency*

Authority to Release Nuclear Weapons

Authorization for the use of nuclear weapons comes from the President of the United States as Commander-in-Chief. In the event of his incapacitation, the line of authority runs to the Vice President and then to the Secretary of Defense, not the Secretary of State.

The means by which the President directs the use of nuclear weapons starts with the so-called **Black Bag** or **Football**, usually carried by an Army Lieutenant Colonel who accompanies the President at all times. The attaché case contains **Gold Codes** (a random jumble of letters and numbers, changed daily by the National Security Agency, and simultaneously delivered to nuclear command posts around the world); the options specified in the **Single Integrated Operational Plan–SIOP** (a plan that accounts for the nuclear weapons of all three branches of the United States military and integrates all the nuclear contingency plans of the regional commands in the Pacific, the Atlantic, and Europe); and the President's decision book containing the instructions for release and execution of the SIOP.

Implementation of the President's decision to release nuclear weapons involves a complex series of steps designed to prevent unauthorized or accidental use.

Under the Constitution of the United States, the Congress has the power to declare war but, as Commander-in-Chief, the President has primary responsibility for the defense of the United States. Recognition of the facts of modern warfare and the existence of nuclear weapons that could strike targets in the United States within minutes led to the enactment of the **War Powers Act** in 1973 giving the President the authority to conduct a war—conventional or nuclear—for 60 days without Congressional approval. Within this period, Congress can take action to terminate use of American forces. The President is required, however, to submit a report to Congress explaining his action within 48 hours of committing American forces into combat. As a practical matter, however, the decision to use nuclear weapons resides within the Executive Branch.

The greatest degree of control and direction exists with respect to the use of intercontinental ballistic missiles and strategic bombers under SAC. The present **National Command and Control System** was created as a result of a conclusion reached in the early 1960's by the Joint Chiefs of Staff who warned Secretary of Defense Robert McNamara that the U.S. early warning and command and control system would not be able to survive a nuclear attack.

The **Command, Control, and Communications** structure (C^3) includes the following:

National Military Command Center (NMCC)—a main operations room located in the Pentagon—is the central facility through which the President would interact with the warning and control system. It has direct communications with all subordinate command centers around the world and has links to the nuclear forces enabling the commanders to deliver Gold Codes directly to missile silos, bomber crews, and submarine commanders.

Alternate Military Command Center (ALMCC)—located deep in a mountain in Pennsylvania (Raven Rock)—is the alternate to the NMCC to be used only in time of nuclear war. Eight miles south is Camp David which also has an underground emergency operations center, that can serve as a nuclear war command post, and is linked by a buried cable to the post in Raven Rock.

North American Aerospace Defense Command (NORAD)—buried deep inside the Cheyenne Mountain in Colorado—is the center where indications and warning information from multiple sources is monitored continuously and relayed to other major command centers. NORAD is an Air Force command effectively linked with SAC but serves as a separate organization with the responsibility for air defense against Soviet attack. This organizational structure does not leave decision-making in the hands of any one organization thus preventing unauthorized or inadvertent use of nuclear weapons.

When Soviet nuclear weapons were carried on bombers rather than missiles, NORAD was created and established as a joint United States/Canada command because the route of Soviet bombers would bring them over Canada. Accordingly, many radars and fighter bases were located in Canada. Because the NORAD weapons were defensive in nature, the NORAD Commander was given a significant delegation of authority to use them, subject to severe restrictions and specific conditions of attack. The weapons he might release would not be of a type that could strike Soviet targets. It is understood, however, that reconsideration of even this limited authorization is underway in the Department of Defense.

Strategic Air Command (SAC)—located in an underground bunker at Offutt Air Force Base in Omaha—has the most effective control with respect to intercontinental ballistic missiles and strategic bomber forces. The SAC Commander has the authority to launch a bomber force to prevent its destruction on the ground by attacking missiles. Once airborne, they hold position awaiting orders from SAC as to whether to proceed or return depending on the threat of the incoming attack which is determined by NORAD. On the SAC Commander's desk is an array of seven different colored telephones with permanently open lines to SAC operations worldwide and to the National Command Authority in Washington.

> **Land-Based Missiles**. On a shelf between the two crewmen in a Minuteman missile silo is the **red box**—an exact replica of those inside the missile submarine command and control center and B-52 cockpits. Secured with two combination locks are the **validation codes** that authenticate the "nuclear control order" and two keys for missiles release. In response to an initial alert command from the SAC controller, an alarm rings inside the capsule and the senior crew member receives an "Emergency Action Message"—an authorized launch instruction from the National Command Authority. The crew commander copies the twelve number and letter code that follows immediately and verifies it with that particular day's launch codes while a hard copy confirmation of the oral message is delivered over a small teletype machine.

Each crew member opens one of the two locks on the red box, removes the sealed "Emergency War Order"—the special instructions for firing the missiles. They also remove their silver firing keys. The launch officers then jointly validate the Emergency Action Message with the launch codes. The crew then waits for the "release message" called the **Nuclear Control Order**.

Before the crews are able to turn their keys to launch their missile, a second crew, in one of the other four launch control centers, must go through the same procedure to validate the launch command; or they can delay and ultimately prevent a launch if they believe it to be the result of an invalid order. The delay lasts for a few minutes and then is automatically cancelled.

Finally, the two crewmen must turn their keys simultaneously and hold them in position for at least five seconds to launch a missile. During this operation, the lit panels on the crewmen's consoles have progressed through launch sequences beginning with "strategic alert" to "warhead armed" to "launch in progress" and ending with "missiles away." Once the missile is fired, there is no recall.

Submarines. The greater difficulty in communicating with our strategic submarines has always posed the risk of accident. The fact that ballistic missile submarines (SSBNs) must often operate thousands of miles from the National Command Centers and are usually cruising deep under water, has required more extensive delegation of release authority. Efforts have been made to improve communication through underground systems in the American midwest. Moreover, the increased range of the Trident I or C4 submarine-launched ballistic missile has significantly ameliorated the communications difficulty. The submarines can now operate much closer to the coast of the United States. The greater security from possible enemy attack and the shorter distance communications must travel provide greater continuity and effectiveness of communications and control.

The issue of authority to use nuclear weapons is a very difficult one because of conflicting considerations. The desirability of a quick response, in some circumstances, would tend toward delegation and the short-cutting of complex procedures. The momentous and fatal consequences of premature and imprudent use of nuclear weapons on the other hand tends toward elaborate and time-consuming procedures.

This conflict has characterized debate about the use of tactical or battlefield nuclear weapons and has led to proposals for creation of a nuclear weapons-free corridor in central Europe. Inevitably, compromises have had to be made and no truly satisfactory system for release and use of nuclear weapons is possible.

Renewed concern about the survivability of the U.S. **Command, Control, and Communications (C³)** led to a decision announced in October 1981 to make further improvements and refinements. The exact nature of these changes is highly classified.

Sources: *U.S. Department of Defense Publications*
U.S. Congressional Committee Reports

Section III

- **The Negotiating Process**

- **The SALT Talks**

    SALT I Agreements
             ABM Treaty
             Interim Agreement on Offensive Weapons

    SALT II Treaty
             Protocol
             Joint Statement of Principles

- **Verification**

- **Existing Treaties and Agreements**

- **Ongoing Arms Control Negotiations**

- **Violation Concerns of the U.S. and U.S.S.R.**

    Prior to 1980
    After 1980

The Negotiating Process

The negotiating positions of the United States on the subject of limiting and reducing nuclear weapons between it and the Soviet Union are discussed and adopted by the National Security Council (NSC) with the participation of the. . .

President
Vice President
Secretary of State
Secretary of Defense
Chairman of the Joint Chiefs of Staff
Director of the Central Intelligence Agency
Director of the U.S. Arms Control & Disarmament Agency
President's National Security Advisor

Position papers are prepared for NSC consideration by an inter-agency working group of government officials representing these agencies.

Although our information on Soviet decision-making is incomplete and uncertain, negotiating positions of the Soviet Union are believed to be determined by the twenty member Politburo, the highest governing group, on the basis of positions developed separately by the relevant agencies. Primarily these agencies are the Ministry of Defense and the Ministry of Foreign Affairs. Any disagreements appear to be resolved at the Politburo level without previous processing by an interagency working group.

The Salt Talks

Strategic arms limitation talks between the United States and the Soviet Union began in 1969 and were conducted—under the acronym *SALT*—during the administrations of three American presidents: Richard Nixon, Gerald Ford, and Jimmy Carter. The purpose of the talks was to promote U.S. national security by reducing the risk of nuclear war through negotiation of mutual limits on strategic nuclear arms.

All three administrations articulated general principles that guided their conduct of negotiations:

- agreements reached should permit the United States to maintain strategic forces at least equal to those of the Soviet Union;
- agreements should maintain and, if possible, enhance the stability of the strategic balance, thereby reducing the likelihood of nuclear war;
- agreements should be adequately verifiable so that Soviet violations of any significance would be detected and acted upon.

When the United States and the Soviet Union were beginning to build a defensive system—the Anti-Ballistic Missile System (ABM)—each side had growing doubts as to whether, in an initial attack, the system would work well enough to prevent attacking missiles from inflicting enormous damage. Both sides recognized that missile defenses, no matter how sophisticated, could still be outsmarted by offensive improvement, and as a consequence spur on the arms race. For this reason, the first phase of the SALT process began in 1969.

Under the direction of President Nixon and National Security Advisor Henry Kissinger, the first results of the SALT process were realized in a *SALT I Agreement* which consisted of two parts—the *ABM Treaty* and the *Interim Agreement*—both concluded in 1972.

Today, there are some who advocate exotic defensive weapons including those based in outer space. But most experts feel that the same problems exist with futuristic weapons as with the ones each superpower worked on when the ABM Treaty was signed. There is no reason to believe that any available or presently foreseeable technology would provide an effective defense against thousands of incoming warheads. Accordingly, the deployment of futuristic weapons would be a destabilizing influence, expensive to deploy, and relatively simple to defeat.

The ABM Treaty

The ABM Treaty, signed in 1972 by the United States and the Soviet Union, was of unlimited duration with joint U.S. and Soviet reviews every five years. The **ABM Treaty** severely limits **defensive systems** designed to intercept and destroy attacking missiles. The Treaty and a Protocol to it limit each side to one ABM installation of not more than 100 missiles and launchers which can be deployed either around an ICBM site or around the national capital.

The ABM Treaty also prohibits development, testing, and deployment of sea-based, air-based, space-based, and mobile land-based ABM systems and their component parts. Some research and development for new ABMs is permitted by the Treaty, but on a very limited scale.

In 1977, the United States and the Soviet Union conducted a review of the ABM Treaty and both sides agreed that the Treaty had operated effectively, continued to serve the interests of both sides, and needed no amendments. The second review was held in 1982, and both countries came to similar conclusions.

The Interim Agreement

The second half of the SALT I accords was an **Interim Agreement on Offensive Weapons.** While the agreement was not a complete freeze on strategic nuclear weapons because it allowed certain replacements and substitutes, it called for a halt to construction of new ICBM silos and placed ceilings on various categories of weapon launchers.

Under the Interim Agreement, both sides were permitted to expand their sea-based missile forces only if they dismantled an equal number of older land- or sea-based missile launchers. Both countries agreed to follow up the Interim Agreement with active negotiations for more comprehensive limitations in the arms race. Thus the Interim Agreement was a holding action to complement the ABM Treaty, to limit competition in **offensive weapons**, and to provide a framework for further negotiations.

Unfortunately, the Interim Agreement counted and limited only the launchers of strategic weapons, not the number of warheads on them. Because multiple-independently-targetable reentry vehicles (MIRVs) were not limited, both sides began to multiply the destructive power of their existing missiles, despite the freeze on launchers. The U.S. began to deploy MIRVs in 1970. The Soviet Union began in 1975.

One of the negotiating options under review by the United States Government in late 1969 and 1970 was a ban on MIRV testing. The idea was that if neither side flight-tested its missiles with MIRVs, neither could have confidence that MIRVs would work as designed. During this time, the Soviet Union was rapidly deploying new land-based and sea-based missiles; the United States was not. Key officials in the Congress and in the Nixon White House felt that MIRVs were necessary to offset the buildup of Soviet missiles. The U.S. had already begun to test MIRVs; the Soviets had not. So these individuals did not wish to give up a clear U.S. advantage.

One concern that was raised at the time was how a MIRV ban could be verified. Officials within the U.S. Arms Control and Disarmament Agency, the Department of State, and the Central Intelligence Agency believed verification by remote devices such as photo-reconnaissance satellites, ground-based radars, and collection of radio transmissions—collectively know as **National Technical Means**—would be adequate. President Nixon and National Security Advisor Kissinger disagreed, as did Pentagon officials. The U.S. proposed that a ban on MIRVs be linked to "on-site inspection" at Soviet missile bases. The Soviets rejected on-site inspection. They proposed that MIRVs be flight-tested but not deployed. But once flight-tested, there was no way to prove that MIRVs were not placed atop missiles except by on-site inspection.

In other words, neither side was sufficiently concerned about MIRVs in the SALT I negotiations to ban or severely limit them.

As a result, within eight years, the Soviets MIRVed about half of their land-based missiles. When these missiles became increasingly accurate, in theory, they placed U.S. land-based missiles at risk—the so-called **window of vulnerability**.

Because the Interim Agreement was intended to be just what its name indicates, it was presented to the Congress as an Executive Agreement, not as a treaty. Of five years duration, the Agreement entered into force on October 3, 1972 and expired on October 3, 1977. At that time, the United States and the Soviet Union separately stated that they did not plan to take any action inconsistent with the provisions of the Interim Agreement pending conclusion of the SALT II negotiations.

SALT II Treaty

Early discussion between the United States and the Soviet Union on a **SALT II Treaty** began in November 1972. It covered a variety of issues including the systems to be limited, the means of establishing equality in strategic nuclear forces, and specific quantitative and qualitative limits. The positions of the two sides differed widely on many of these questions, and only limited progress was made in the first two years.

A major breakthrough occurred in November 1974 at the Vladivostok meeting between President Gerald Ford and the Soviet leader, Leonid Brezhnev. They agreed on basic guidelines for a SALT II agreement and a common ceiling of 2400 strategic weapon launchers per side of which no more than 1320 could be launchers of MIRVed missiles.

Finally, after almost five more years of difficult negotiations, an agreement was reached that accommodated both the Soviet desire to retain the Vladivostok framework for an agreement and the U.S. desire for more comprehensive limitations.

The SALT II Agreement consists of three parts:

- a **Treaty** which would incorporate and reduce the limits of the Vladivostok accord and which would be in force through 1985;

- a **Protocol** that would prohibit through 1981 the deployment of weapons about which both sides had the greatest difficulty in agreeing—ground-launched and sea-launched cruise missiles and mobile ICBMS; and

- a **Joint Statement of Principles**—an agreed set of guidelines for further negotiations.

The **SALT II Treaty** was completed and signed by President Carter and President Brezhnev in Vienna on June 18, 1979. The Treaty has not been ratified by the U.S. Senate but is still tacitly honored by both sides.

The SALT II Treaty, the most detailed and far-reaching agreement in the history of nuclear arms control, was to be in effect through December 1985. It provided for:

- a limit of 2250 (down from 2400 at Vladivostok) on the total number of strategic nuclear delivery vehicles, namely;

ICBMs   InterContinental Ballistic Missiles

SLBMs   Submarine-Launched Ballistic Missiles

HEAVY BOMBERS including those carrying long-range cruise missiles

Within the total ceiling of 2250, each side has the right to determine the number of weapons it prefers to have within each category, but with the following limitations:

- within this 2250 ceiling, the total number of

MIRVed ICBMs)
MIRVed SLBMs)   could not exceed 1320
HEAVY BOMBERS)
   (with ALCMs)

- within this 1320 limit, the total number of

MIRVed ICBMs)   could not exceed 1200
MIRVed SLBMs)

- within this 1200 limit, the total number of

MIRVed ICBMs)   could not exceed 820

- within this 820 limit, the Soviet Union was limited to 308 "heavy missiles" (SS-18s)

The agreement also provides for:

- a ban on construction of additional fixed ICBM launchers and on the modifications each side can make to existing ICBMs;

- a ban on flight-testing or deployment of new types of ICBMs; except for one new land-based missile with a limit of 10 warheads;

- a ban on increasing the number of warheads on existing types of land-based ICBMs; a limit of 14 warheads on sea-based SLBMs;
- a limit on the average number of long-range cruise missiles to 28 on each side's bomber force; with a limit of 20 on existing heavy bombers (B-52s);
- a ban on the production, testing, and deployment of the Soviet SS-16 missile designed for mobile launchers, including a ban on the production of that missile's components;
- an exchange of data on the systems included in the various SALT-limited categories in order to establish an agreed base to measure reductions.

The **Protocol** to the Treaty was to remain in force through December 31, 1981. It placed temporary limits on those systems not yet ready for long-term resolution:

- a ban on deployment of mobile ICBM launchers and flight-testing of ICBMs from such launchers. Development of such systems, short of flight-testing, is permitted. (Mobile launchers were recognized to present troubling verification problems, but the United States wanted to keep options open for deploying the MX after the Protocol expired.)
- a ban on deployment, but not testing, of land-based and sea-based cruise missiles with ranges in excess of 375 miles. (The United States wanted to preserve the right to deploy these weapons. The Soviets wanted to ban such cruise missiles for the term of the Treaty, but eventually accepted the shorter-term limit on deployment.)

The **Joint Statement of Principles**, the third element of the SALT II Agreement, established a basic framework for the next stage of SALT negotiations, SALT III. Both countries agreed on the following general goals to be achieved in the next round of talks.

- further reductions in the number of strategic weapon launchers;
- further qualitative limits on strategic weapon bombers;
- resolution of the issues addressed in the Protocol.

Sources: "SALT II Agreement," Selected Documents No. 12A
U.S. Department of State
"1980, 1981, 1982, Annual Reports,"
U.S. Arms Control and Disarmament Agency

Verification

As used in the vocabulary of arms control, *verification* means the process of determining whether there has been compliance with the provisions of arms control treaties and agreements. It is the attempt to make sure that, through the application of modern intelligence techniques, certain activities prohibited by a treaty are in fact *not* taking place.

Monitoring—the collection of intelligence data—is the initial stage in the verification process. When the data are obtained, they must be evaluated with a view to the provisions of a particular agreement, and evidence must be assembled for possible noncompliance. The evidence as a whole serves as the basis for deciding whether an issue of violation is involved. Since data with respect to compliance may be subject to differing interpretations, judgment and decision at the political level is frequently required.

Once nuclear weapons became a part of national arsenals, their unprecedented destructive power made it imperative to seek international agreement on the limitation and reduction of arms. Yet the potential for concealment of nuclear devices, together with the speed with which nuclear weapons can reach their targets, and the difficulty of defense in a period of rapid development of missile technology, make effective verification of agreements both difficult and necessary.

In 1946, the **Baruch Plan**, the first American proposal for the control of nuclear weapons presented to the United Nations, called for an international agency to own and supervise the production of nuclear materials solely for peaceful purposes. It proposed a continuing system of inspection to guard against the illicit production and stockpiling of nuclear weapons. The Soviet government objected to the extent of its provisions on inspection and control, and Soviet counterproposals were regarded by the United States and other nations as wholly inadequate for verification purposes.

By 1955, the United States and the Soviet Union had come to acknowledge that any accounting of nuclear weapons and materials already produced would be extremely difficult to verify. This, along with the inability to determine the extent of proliferation of such weapons to other countries, meant that complete elimination of such weapons was not a practicable goal for the foreseeable future. Accordingly, attention began to focus on the possibilities of limitation and reduction with measures that would facilitate them such as a ban on nuclear testing and steps to avert the danger of surprise attack.

At a conference in Geneva that same year, President Eisenhower proposed an **Open Skies Plan** which called for inspection of United States and Soviet territory by aircraft of the other side as a warning system against surprise attack. The Soviet Union rejected this plan. However, the concept of this type of inspection, on a bilateral basis rather than under the auspices of an international body, was put into practical use in the 18-nation *Antarctic Treaty of 1959*. Under the terms of this treaty, all parties, including the Soviet Union, agreed to open their installations on that continent to inspection by any of the other signatory nations.

In 1958, a meeting in Geneva of technical experts from the West and the Soviet bloc concluded that a complete ban on nuclear testing could be adequately verified by the existing techniques of seismic monitoring with on-site inspections to clear up ambiguous cases. It also recommended establishing a network of monitoring posts, under international authority, in the territory of the nuclear powers and in conveniently situated third countries.

Later that year, experts met in Geneva to consider possible techniques for monitoring military deployments in order to detect preparations of surprise attack. At this conference, the Soviet Union proposed a warning system involving aerial reconnaissance as well as ground observation posts along the East-West border. Technical possibilities of photographic and radar reconnaissance by orbiting space satellites were first being explored at this time.

In the following years, efforts to negotiate a comprehensive test ban involving on-site inspections and an international system of verification proved unsuccessful. Concerns about the adequacy of techniques for monitoring underground tests at long range and opposition from proponents of further nuclear weapons development prevented negotiations of a comprehensive ban.

In September 1961, the United States and Great Britain proposed a ban on atmospheric nuclear tests that would be monitored solely by "existing means of detection." These would include photographic, radar and electronic surveillance capabilities; seismic instrumentation that detects location and magnitude of underground nuclear explosions; air sampling systems of high sensitivity; and advanced techniques for the analysis and evaluation of the data collected. An agreement was eventually reached on a ban on nuclear testing in the atmosphere, under water, and in outer space. The **Limited Test Ban Treaty of 1963**, which relied solely on **national technical means** of verification for monitoring compliance, marked an important step in the history of arms control.

It was recognized, however, that verification of strategic weapons limitations would present greater difficulties and involve greater uncertainties than verification of the Limited Test Ban Treaty. In 1967, the United States and the Soviet Union decided to pursue the possibilities of an agreement on strategic nuclear weapons by also relying on **national technical means**.

In 1972, the SALT I agreements were concluded. Both the **Anti-Ballistic Missile Treaty** (ABM Treaty) and the **Interim Agreement on Strategic Offensive Arms** explicitly provided for verification by **national technical means** at each party's disposal to assure compliance. Each party also agreed not to interfere with the means of verification of the other, and each party agreed not to use deliberate concealment measures which impede verification.

In addition to these provisions, the **Standing Consultative Commission** (SCC) was established as a joint U.S. U.S.S.R. body charged with promoting implementation of the objectives and provisions of the ABM Treaty and the Interim Agreement as well as the Agreement on Measures to Reduce the Risk of Outbreak of Nuclear War which was negotiated during SALT I and entered into force on September 30, 1971.

Generally, the Commission is responsible for considering questions of compliance with obligations assumed by the U.S. and the U.S.S.R. under those agreements, for reconciling any misunderstandings or uncertainties arising in the performance of those obligations, and for considering proposals for increasing the viability of those agreements. The regulations that govern the SCC's internal operation provide that the proceedings of the Commission shall be private. This has facilitated the direct and frank exchanges concerning strategic weapons systems and other matters related to SALT agreement implementation which are necessary for the SCC to carry out effectively its assigned responsibilities. Each component of the Commission operates under instructions and guidance from the highest levels of its government. It is clearly understood between them that each SCC Commissioner keeps his government fully informed in accordance with the pertinent procedures and process of that government. The Commission holds periodic sessions in Geneva at least twice annually and may be convened for additional sessions at the request of either Commissioner. In between sessions, the Commissioners may communicate with one another through diplomatic channels.

In November 1972, the second phase of the SALT Talks aimed at achieving a more comprehensive agreement on strategic offensive arms to replace the Interim Agreement, began and culminated with the signing of the **SALT II Treaty** in June 1979. This treaty covered the systems to be limited, the means of establishing equality in strategic nuclear forces, and specific quantitative and qualitative limits. Adequate verification has been a key objective of SALT and is an essential feature of SALT II.

For each provision and the agreement as a whole, the relevant question is whether or not compliance with the limits can be determined to the extent necessary to safeguard our security. Could we identify an attempted evasion, if it occurs on a scale large enough to pose a significant military risk, in time to make an appropriate response? Meeting this test is what is meant by the term **adequate verification.** In 1980, the Secretary of Defense, the Secretary of State, and the Chairman of the Joint Chiefs of Staff have all testified that compliance with the provisions of the SALT II Treaty is adequately verifiable.

There have been disputes as to whether or not the Soviets have complied with the SALT accords. During the Nixon, Ford, and Carter administrations, every U.S. concern raised at the SCC was resolved to the satisfaction of these Presidents: either the practices in question stopped, or they were clarified in a way that alleviated U.S. concerns.

Critics of the SALT agreements dispute this record maintaining that Soviet violations occurred, and that previous administrations were not forthright in their handling of them. The Reagan Administration has been more inclined to adopt this view. Compliance issues continue to arise during the Reagan Administration. To some, the

Kremlin is simply continuing its standard practice of testing at the margins of agreements reached. To others, the Kremlin is becoming more bold in its practices.

Unquestionably, it became harder to resolve SALT compliance questions after 1979. U.S.-Soviet relations steadily worsened, and SALT II compliance questions were aggravated by the U.S. failure to ratify the SALT II Treaty. ABM compliance issues were complicated by President Reagan's endorsement of a futuristic defense against nuclear attack. Moreover, there was disturbing evidence that the U.S.S.R. was engaged in chemical and biological warfare activities, despite treaty obligations to the contrary. These incidents—the alleged use of "Yellow Rain" in Afghanistan and Southeast Asia as well as an outbreak of anthrax in a Soviet city in which a military compound suspected of biological warfare activities was located—cast a pall over ongoing arms control negotiations of every kind.

Sources: "Verification: The Critical Element of Arms Control,"
U.S. Arms Control and Disarmament Agency

"SALT ONE: Compliance," - "SALT TWO: Verification,"
U.S. Department of State

"1980, 1981, 1982 Annual Reports,"
U.S. Arms Control and Disarmament Agency

Existing Treaties and Agreements

To prevent the spread of nuclear weapons . . .

1959 Antarctic Treaty—demilitarizes the Antarctic and declares that it shall be used for peaceful purposes.

1967 Outer Space Treaty—prohibits placing nuclear or other weapons of mass destruction in outer space and outlaws the establishment of military bases, installations, and fortifications, the testing of any type of weapons, and the conduct of military maneuvers in outer space.

1967 Treaty of Tlatelolco—prohibits the testing, use, manufacture, production or acquisition by any means of nuclear weapons in Latin America. Under Protocol II the nuclear weapons states agree to respect the military denuclearization of Latin America.

1968 Non-Proliferation Treaty—prohibits the transfer of nuclear weapons by nuclear weapon states and the acquisition of such weapons by adhering non-nuclear weapon states.

1971 Seabed Treaty—prohibits the placement of nuclear weapons or other weapons of mass destruction on the seabed beyond a 12-mile zone.

To reduce the risk of nuclear war . . . (agreements between the U.S. and U.S.S.R. only)

1963 Hot Line Agreement—establishes a direct communications link between the United States and the Soviet Union for use in time of emergency. A 1971 agreement further improved the communications link.

1971 Nuclear Accidents Agreement—provides for immediate notification by the United States and the Soviet Union of an accidental, unauthorized incident, or a possible detonation of a nuclear weapon.

1973 Agreement on Prevention of Nuclear War—provides that the United States and the Soviet Union will take all actions necessary to prevent the outbreak of nuclear war.

To limit nuclear testing . . .

1963 Limited Test Ban Treaty—bans nuclear weapon tests in the atmosphere, in outer space, and under water.

1974 Threshold Test Ban Treaty*—limits the yield of underground U.S. and Soviet nuclear weapons tests to 150 kilotons.

1976 Peaceful Nuclear Explosions Treaty*—complements the 1974 Threshold Test Ban Treaty by prohibiting any individual underground nuclear explosion for peaceful purposes which has a yield of more than 150 kilotons, or any group explosion with a total yield greater than 1500 kilotons.

To limit nuclear weapons . . . (between the U.S. and U.S.S.R. only)

1972 ABM Treaty (SALT I)—limits the deployment of anti-ballistic missile defenses by the United States and the Soviet Union.

1972 Interim Agreement (SALT I)—freezes the aggregate number of U.S. and Soviet ballistic missile launchers for a five-year period.

1979 SALT II Treaty*—limits numbers of strategic nuclear delivery vehicles, launchers of MIRVed missiles, bombers with long range cruise missiles, warheads on existing ICBMs etc. Bans testing or deploying new ICBMs.

Other . . .

1925 Geneva Protocol—bans the use in war of asphyxiating, poisonous, or other gases, and of bacteriological methods of warfare.

1972 Biological Weapons Convention—bans the development, production, and stockpiling of biological and toxin weapons; requires the destruction of stocks.

1975 Conference on Security and Cooperation in Europe (CSCE)—contains a provision on confidence-building measures which provides for notification of major military maneuvers in Europe.

1977 Environmental Modification Convention—prohibits the hostile use of techniques which could produce substantial environmental modifications.

1981 Inhumane Weapons Convention*—bans use of fragmentation bombs not detectable in the human body; bans use against civilians of mines, booby traps, and incendiary weapons; requires record-keeping mines.

*not ratified

Ongoing Arms Control Negotiations

Initiated in 1961
Conference of the Committee on Disarmament (CCD)
the central forum dealing with multilateral arms control to discuss general and complete disarmament.

Initiated in 1979
Committee on Disarmament (CD)
created by the 1978 U.N. Special Session on Disarmament; this replaced the Conference of the Committee on Disarmament above.

Initiated in 1973
Mutual and Balanced Force Reductions (MBFR)
multilateral negotiations seeking to limit NATO and Warsaw Pact forces within a limited geographic region.

Initiated in 1978
Comprehensive Test Ban Negotiations (CTB)[1]
talks between the United States, the Soviet Union, and Great Britain which seek to end all nuclear weapon tests.

Initiated in 1981
Intermediate Nuclear Forces (INF)[2]
talks between the United States and the Soviet Union on limiting intermediate-range missiles in Europe.

Initiated in 1982
Strategic Arms Reduction Talks (START)[3]
talks between the United States and the Soviet Union on the limitations of strategic nuclear weapons (name changed from SALT to START)

[1]The Reagan Administration suspended these negotiations.

[2]The Soviets suspended these negotiations in December, 1983.

[3]These negotiations were deadlocked as of December, 1983 when the Soviets declined to set a date for their resumption.

Source: "Arms Control and Disarmament Agreements,"
U.S. Arms Control and Disarmament Agency

Violation Concerns
Questions Raised by the United States

PRIOR TO 1980

Launch Control Facilities (Special Purpose Silos)

Under Article I of the 1972 Interim Agreement, **the Parties undertake not to start construction of additional fixed land-based intercontinental ballistic missile (ICBM) launchers.**

In 1973, the United States observed excavations at a number of launch sites in the U.S.S.R. If these had been intended to contain ICBMs, they would have constituted a violation. In response to the United States' concern, the U.S.S.R. stated that the excavations were for launch control purposes. As additional intelligence became available, the United States concluded that the silos were indeed designed to serve a launch control function.

Modern Large Ballistic Missiles (SS-19 Issue)

Under Article II of the Interim Agreement, **conversion of land-based launchers for light ICBMs into land-based launchers for heavy ICBMs is prohibited.**

In 1975 when deployment of the SS-19 began, its size caused the United States some concern. Since the U.S. and the U.S.S.R. had not come to an agreement on a quantitative definition of a "heavy" ICBM which would constrain increases in the size of Soviet "light" ICBMs, this was not a violation of the agreement. The Soviet Union had refused to agree to specifications for new ICBMs and the U.S. statement to that effect was unilateral and not binding on the Soviet Union. However, the U.S. purpose in raising this issue with the U.S.S.R. was to emphasize the importance that the United States attached to the distinction between light and heavy ICBMs. Further discussions of this question in the SCC forum were deferred because it was under active consideration in the SALT II negotiations. Since that time, the U.S. and the U.S.S.R. delegations have agreed on a clear demarcation in terms of missile launch-weight and throw-weight between "light" and "heavy" ICBMs in the text of SALT II.

Soviet Dismantling or Destruction of Replaced ICBM Launchers

Under Article III of the Interim Agreement and the Protocol thereto, **the Soviets had to dismantle 51 replaced launchers by early 1976 in accordance with the agreed procedures developed in the SCC.**

When it became apparent that the Soviets had not completed all the required dismantling actions on time according to SCC procedures, the U.S. decided to raise the question with the Soviets. But before the U.S. could do so, the Soviets had acknowledged in the SCC that the dismantling of 41 older ICBM launchers had not been completed in the required time period and predicted completion by June 1976. It also agreed to the U.S. demand that no more submarines with replacement SLBM launchers begin sea trials prior to such completion. Both conditions were met. Although the U.S. has observed some minor procedural discrepancies at a number of these deactivated launch sites and at others as the replacement process continued, all launchers have been in a condition that satisfied the essential substantive requirements which are that they cannot be used to launch missiles and cannot be reactivated in a short time.

Concealment Measures

Under Article V of the Interim Agreement and Article XII of the ABM Treaty, **interference with the national technical means of verification and use of deliberate concealment measures that impede verification by national technical means are prohibited.**

In 1974, the extent of concealment activities in the U.S.S.R. increased substantially. None of them prevented U.S. verification of compliance with the provisions of the ABM Treaty or the Interim Agreement, but the concern was that they could impede verification in the future if the pattern of concealment measures was permitted to expand. The United States stated its concern and in early 1975, careful analysis of intelligence information led to the conclusion that there no longer appeared to be an expanding pattern of concealment activities associated with strategic weapons programs in the U.S.S.R.

Denial of Test Information

Under Article V of the Interim Agreement, **encoding missile-test telemetry that impedes verification is a violation.**

During the SALT II negotiations, it was reported that the Soviets were engaged in encoding missile-test telemetry. If this activity had impeded verification of compliance with agreement provisions, this activity would be considered a violation. Prior to 1981, it was agreed that this was not the case.

Antisatellite Systems

Under Article V of the Interim Agreement and Article XII of the ABM Treaty, **actual use of an ASAT system against U.S. national technical means of verification is prohibited.**

It has been alleged that Soviet development of antisatellite systems is a violation of the obligation not to interfere with national technical means of verification of compliance with SALT provisions. Since development of such systems is not prohibited, and since the U.S. recently has tested an ASAT system, such development does not constitute violation of existing agreements. The actual use of an ASAT system against verification satellites is prohibited, but this has not occurred.

Blinding U.S. Satellites

Under Article V of the Interim Agreement and Article XII of the ABM Treaty, **interference with or deliberate concealment measures which impede verification by national technical means of compliance with provisions of the agreement is prohibited.**

In 1975, information suggested possible Soviet use of something like laser energy to "blind" certain U.S. satellites, an activity inconsistent with the obligations of the Interim Agreement and the ABM Treaty. When it was thoroughly analyzed, it was determined that no questionable Soviet activity was involved and that U.S. monitoring capabilities had not been affected. The analysis indicated that the phenomena had resulted from several large fires caused by breaks along natural gas pipelines in the U.S.S.R.

Concealment at Test Range

Under Article V of the Interim Agreement, **deliberate concealment measures are prohibited.**

In 1977, the U.S. observed the use of a large screen over an ICBM launcher undergoing conversion at a test range in the U.S.S.R. The U.S. expressed the view that the use of a covering over an ICBM silo launcher concealed activities from national technical means of verification and could impede verification of compliance with provisions of the Interim Agreement, specifically, the provision which deals with increases in dimensions of ICBM silo launchers. Although the Soviets took the position that the provisions of the Interim Agreement were not applicable to the activity in question, they subsequently removed the net covering.

Mobile ICBMs

Under the Interim Agreement, **development and testing of a mobile ICBM is not prohibited but a unilateral statement of the U.S. expressed the view that deployment of such systems would be inconsistent with the objectives of the agreement.**

The suspicion that the Soviet SS-20, a mobile intermediate-range ballistic missile system, might have ICBM range capabilities has proven to be inaccurate. It is judged to be capable of reaching the Aleutian Islands and western Alaska from eastern U.S.S.R.; however, it cannot reach the contiguous 48 States from any of its likely deployment areas. Although the range capability of any missile system can be extended by reducing the total weight of its payload or adding another propulsion state, there is no evidence that the SS-20 has been tested with such modifications. The U.S. would be able to detect the necessary intercontinental-range testing of such a modified system.

Soviet ABM Radar on Kamchatka Peninsula

*Under Article IV of the ABM Treaty, **only those ABM components used for development or testing at current or additionally agreed ranges are permitted.***

In 1975, the United States identified what seemed to be a new radar on Kamchatka Peninsula which it believed might constitute the establishment of a new Soviet ABM Test Range. When the U.S. brought this to the attention of the Soviet side, however, the U.S.S.R. indicated that a range with a radar instrumentation complex had existed on the Kamchatka Peninsula on the date of signature of the ABM Treaty. It was therefore stated by the U.S.S.R. and accepted by the U.S. that Kamchatka and Sary Shagan would be the only ABM test ranges in the U.S.S.R.

Soviet Reporting of Dismantling of Excess ABM Test Launchers

*Under Article IV and Article VIII of the ABM Treaty, **each side is limited to no more than 15 ABM launchers at test ranges.***

In 1974, the U.S.S.R. notified the SCC that its excess ABM launchers had been dismantled in accordance with the agreed procedures worked out in the SCC. Because several of these launchers had been deactivated prior to entry into force of the agreed SCC procedures and not in accordance with such procedures, the U.S. raised the matter as a case of inaccurate notification or reporting. Although their reactivation would not be of strategic significance, the issue was raised by the United States so that in the future care would be taken to insure that notification as well as dismantling or destruction was to be in strict accordance with agreed procedures.

Mobile ABM

*Under Article V of the ABM Treaty, **development, testing, or deployment of a mobile ABM system or a mobile ABM radar is prohibited.***

Questions have been raised about possible Soviet development of a mobile ABM system. Since 1971, the Soviets have installed at ABM test ranges several radars associated with ABM systems currently in development. One type of radar associated with this system can be erected in a matter of months, rather than years as has been the case. Another type could be emplaced on prepared concrete foundations which can be installed more rapidly than previous ABM systems. But they are not judged mobile in the sense of being able to move about readily or to be hidden. The U.S. recognizes that the U.S.S.R. does not have a mobile ABM system or components for such a system.

Possible Testing of an Air Defense System (SA-5) Radar in an ABM Mode

*Under Article VI of the ABM Treaty, **missiles, launchers or radars other than ABM interceptor missiles, ABM launchers, or ABM radars cannot be given capabilities to counter strategic ballistic missiles or their elements in flight trajectory.***

In 1973 and 1974, U.S. observation of Soviet tests of ballistic missiles led to the belief that a radar associated with the SA-5 surface to air missile system had been used to track strategic missiles during flight. Even though much more testing in a significantly different form would be needed before the Soviets could achieve an ABM capability for the SA-5, and extensive and observable modifications to other components of the system would have been necessary, the activity was ambiguous. The United States raised this issue but the Soviets maintained that no Soviet air defense radar had been tested in an ABM mode. They also noted that the use of non-ABM radars for range safety or instrumentation purposes was not limited by the ABM Treaty. A short time later, the radar activity that caused concern had ceased.

AFTER 1980

Krasnoyarsk Radar

*Under Article VI of the ABM Treaty, **each Party undertakes not to deploy radars for early warning of strategic ballistic missile attack except at locations along the periphery of its national territory and oriented outward.***

Early in 1983, the Soviets began construction of a phased-array radar near Krasnoyarsk approximately 500 miles from the Soviet border, north of Mongolia and oriented northeastward. The United States reportedly contends that the Krasnoyarsk radar is similar in appearance to other Soviet early warning radars, that it is not located "along the periphery," and not oriented outward since its principal area of coverage is the Siberian land mass. The Soviets contend that the radar is for tracking satellites. Because of the location and orientation of the radar and because it does not share the technical characteristics of other radars used exclusively for tracking satellites, the United States has not accepted the Soviet interpretation.

Encoding of Missile Test Data

*Under Article XV of the SALT II Treaty, **each Party is free to use various methods of transmitting telemetric information during testing including encryption except that neither Party shall engage in deliberate denial of telemetric information when such denial impedes verification of compliance with the provisions of the Treaty.***

When being tested, a missile transmits radio signals to ground monitoring stations so that its performance can be assessed. These signals are also monitored by listening devices of the other side for military intelligence and arms control. Over the last several years, it has been reported that the Soviets have used a high level of encryption in the testing of their new SLBM, the SS-X-20, and in testing the SS-X-24 and SS-X-25 ICBMs. Some reports put the level as high as 60–100% being encrypted during certain tests. What is important, however, is not how many channels are being encoded but which ones. Only when channels are blocked so as to impede ability to verify Soviet compliance with SALT II could a violation be alleged. The Soviets contend this is not the case. The U.S. has multiple redundant capabilities for gathering intelligence on missile tests, other than monitoring telemetry.

Banned Deployment of SS-16

*Under a Common Understanding in Article IV of the SALT II Treaty, **the U.S.S.R. agreed not to produce, test, or deploy ICBMs of the SS-16 type, and in particular, not to produce the SS-16 third stage, or the reentry vehicle of that missile.***

While admitting that the evidence is ambiguous and that a definite conclusion cannot be reached, the U.S. government contends that there is evidence of activities at Plesetsk that may constitute a violation of this provision of the treaty. Concerns over SS-16 deployment were expressed during the Carter Administration although evidence was not deemed sufficient to raise this matter at the SCC.

Exceeding the Limits of the Threshold Test Ban Treaty (TTBT)

*Under Article I of the Threshold Test Ban Treaty, **the Parties undertake to prohibit, to prevent, and not to carry out any underground nuclear weapon test having a yield exceeding 150 kilotons at any place under its jurisdiction or control.***

In 1974, the U.S., U.S.S.R. and the United Kingdom signed the Threshold Test Ban Treaty which prohibits testing nuclear devices underground with an explosive power (yield) of greater than 150 kilotons. They also agreed that one or two breaches would not be considered a violation. While the evidence is ambiguous and no definitive conclusions have been reached, it has been alleged that since 1978, the U.S.S.R. has conducted 14 underground tests above the 150 kiloton limit and that several were about 250 kilotons. To calculate yield of Soviet tests, seismographs in various locations around the world, record the seismic waves that underground nuclear explosions generate. Exact calculation is difficult particularly because the TTBT and its companion Treaty on Peaceful Nuclear Explosions have not been ratified and therefore the provisions to exchange data have not become operative. Imprecisions in yield estimates increase when recording seismic signals at great distances and because seismologists use various methods to adjust for the many variables. Seismologists at the Defense Advanced Research Agency (DARPA) determined that 2 U.S. tests and 9 Soviet tests had seismic signals larger than expected for 150 kilotons.

Violation Concerns
Questions Raised by the U.S.S.R.

PRIOR TO 1980

Shelters over Minuteman Silos

Under Article V of the Interim Agreement, *deliberate concealment measures which impede verification of compliance by national technical means are prohibited.*

Beginning in 1974, the United States used prefabricated shelters of about 2700 square feet over Minuteman silos to provide environmental protection during modernization and silo-hardening work. The Soviets classified the activity as deliberate concealment. Based on the nature of the shelters and their intended use for protection of workers, and not for concealment, the United States contended that their use was consistent with the provisions of the Interim Agreement. In 1977, the U.S. modified the use of these shelters by reducing their size by almost 50 percent.

Radar on Shemya Island

Under Article III of the ABM Treaty, *ABM systems or their components can be deployed only within one ABM deployment area centered on the Party's national capital and within one deployment area containing ICBM silo launchers.*

In 1973, the United States began construction of a new phased-array radar on Shemya Island, Alaska to be used for national technical means of verification, space tracking, and early warning. In 1975, the Soviets raised the question whether the radar was an ABM radar which would not be permitted at this location according to the provisions of the ABM Treaty. The United States discussed this matter and eliminated any concern about possible inconsistency with the provisions of the ABM Treaty, and it became operational in early 1977.

Dismantling or Destruction of the ABM Radar under Construction at Malmstrom AFB

Under Article III and Article VIII of the ABM Treaty, *only one ABM system deployment area is permitted for defense of ICBM.*

In 1972, the United States had ABM defenses under construction in two deployment areas containing ICBM silos. Since the ABM Treaty permitted each party only one such ABM system, the United States immediately halted the construction in Malmstrom AFB, Montana according to specific procedures for dismantling or destruction. In 1974, the U.S. notified the U.S.S.R. in the SCC that Malmstrom dismantling activities had been completed. The Soviets raised a question about one detailed aspect which they felt had not been carried out in full accord with the agreement procedures. The U.S. reviewed the actions taken to dismantle the Malmstrom site and showed photographs of the before and after conditions. The question was resolved on that basis.

Atlas and Titan I Launchers

Under a protocol developed by the Standing Consultative Commission, *replacement, dismantling, and destruction of strategic offensive arms must be governed by the detailed procedures of the SCC.*

In 1966, the United States deactivated 177 launchers for the obsolete Atlas and Titan I ICBM systems according to SCC protocol. In 1975, the Soviets apparently perceived an ambiguity with respect to the status and conditions of these launchers based on the amount of dismantling which had been done, and its effect on their possible reactivation time. The U.S. view was that these launchers were obsolete and deactivated prior to the Interim Agreement, and therefore were not subject to the accompanying dismantling or destruction procedures of that agreement. However, we did provide some information on their condition illustrating that they could not be reactivated easily or quickly. The discussion ceased in mid-1975.

Privacy of SCC Proceedings

Under the Standing Consultative Commission Regulations-Paragraph 8, **proceedings of the SCC shall be conducted in private and can be made public only with the express consent of both Commissioners.**

Prior to the special SCC session held in early 1975 to discuss certain questions related to compliance, several articles appeared in various U.S. publications speculating about the possibility of certain Soviet violations of the SALT agreements purported to be from accurate intelligence information. The Soviets expressed their concern about the importance of confidentiality in the work of the SCC and were apparently particularly concerned about press items that may appear to have official U.S. government sanction. The United States discussed the usefulness of maintaining privacy of our negotiations and limiting speculation in the public media on SCC proceedings, but at the same time expressed the need to keep the public adequately informed.

AFTER 1980

Deadlocked Arms Control Talks

Under Article VI of the NonProliferation Treaty, **the Parties undertake to pursue negotiations in good faith on effective measures relating to cessation of the nuclear arms race at an early date and to nuclear disarmament, and on a treaty on general and complete disarmament under strict and effective international control.**

The U.S.S.R. charges the U.S. with violating the obligation to conduct arms control talks in "a spirit of good will." It blames the U.S. for the arms control stalemate, for failing to ratify the SALT II Treaty, and for unilaterally discontinuing talks on the general and complete prohibition of nuclear weapon tests, on Indian Ocean naval force restraints, and on anti-satellite systems.

Deployment of Missiles in Europe

Under Article XII and XIII of the SALT II Treaty, **each Party undertakes not to circumvent the provisions of the Treaty through any other state or states or in any other manner, and not to assume any international obligations which would conflict with this Treaty.**

The U.S.S.R. claims that the U.S. deployment in western Europe of nuclear arms— the Pershing II ballistic missiles and long-range cruise missiles capable of reaching targets in the U.S.S.R.—are additions to the U.S. strategic offensive arsenal and therefore a violation of these provisions of the SALT II Treaty. In the light of this deployment, the Soviet Union questions the credibility of the U.S. statement that "it would refrain from any actions undermining existing agreements on strategic arms," even though the Treaty had not been ratified.

Shelters over Minuteman Silos

Under Article V of the Interim Agreement, **deliberate concealment measures which impede verification of compliance by national technical means is prohibited.**

The Soviet Union states that it has repeatedly raised the question of shelters over the Minuteman II and Titan II missile launchers. They classify this activity as deliberate concealment of work to refit launchers of the Minuteman II, and claim that once refitted, these launchers do not differ in practical terms from the launchers of Minuteman III missiles. They further conjecture that MIRVed Minuteman III missiles are being deployed in these silos which would also constitute a violation of the SALT II Treaty limiting the number of MIRVed ICBMs. The question of these shelters had been previously raised and considered resolved by the reduction in their size.

Privacy of SCC Proceedings

Under the Standing Consultative Commission Regulations, Paragraph 8, **proceedings of the SCC shall be conducted in private and can be made public only with the express consent of both Commissioners.**

The U.S.S.R. continues to express concern about alleged U.S. violation of the confidentiality of SCC discussions. The U.S.S.R. insists that this must be stopped.

Abiding by the Protocol of the SALT II Treaty

*Under the Protocol to the SALT II Treaty, **the deployment of weapons about which both sides had the greatest difficulty in agreeing—ground-launched and sea-launched cruise missiles and mobile ICBMs—is prohibited.***

The Soviets contend that there has been accelerated development of new strategic offensive forces such as the MX, Midgetman, nuclear-powered submarines armed with Trident missiles, B-1B and Stealth strategic bombers, multi-purpose shuttle space systems, and long-range air, sea, and land-based cruise missiles. They claim that this is in violation of the Protocol to the SALT II Treaty and contradicts the recognized principles of international law as well as fundamental Soviet-American accords—which clearly stipulate that neither side shall strive for military superiority and shall be guided by the principal of equal security.

Exceeding the Limits of the Threshold Test Ban Treaty

*Under Article I of the Threshold Test Ban Treaty, **the Parties undertake to prohibit, to prevent, and not to carry out any underground nuclear weapon test having a yield exceeding 150 kilotons at any place under its jurisdiction or control.***

According to data gathered by the U.S.S.R., the United States is charged with violating the Treaty by continuing to test nuclear devices underground over the yield of 150 kilotons.

Radioactive Debris

*Under Article I of the Limited Test Ban Treaty of 1963, **the Parties are prohibited from testing nuclear weapons in the atmosphere, outer space, or under water, or any other environment if the explosion causes radioactive debris to be present outside the territorial limits of the State under whose jurisdiction or control such explosion is conducted.***

The U.S.S.R. says it has approached the U.S. about the ejection of radioactive substances beyond the national territorial limits of the U.S. as a result of underground nuclear explosions. They also claim that the U.S. has refused to conduct talks on the conclusion of an agreement on general and complete prohibition of nuclear weapon tests as well as rejecting the Soviet proposed moratorium on all nuclear weapon tests.

Radar Shemya Island and PAVE PAW Radars

*Under Article III and Article VI of the ABM Treaty, **ABM systems or their components can be deployed only within one ABM deployment area centered on the Party's national capital and within one deployment area containing ICBM silo launchers; each Party undertakes not to give missiles, launchers, or radars, other than ABM interceptor missiles, ABM launchers, or ABM radars, capabilities to counter strategic ballistic missiles or their elements in flight trajectory, and not to test them in an ABM mode.***

In 1973, the question of a radar station on Shemya Island was raised by the Soviets, and the U.S. interpretation that its use was for verification, space-tracking, and early warning purposes was accepted. The U.S.S.R. now claims that this radar station has radar system elements that can be utilized for ABM purposes; that shelters were used over anti-missile launcher silos; that work is being conducted to create mobile ABM radar systems and space-based ABM systems; that the Minuteman I ICBMs are being tested for anti-missile capabilities; and that multiple warheads are being developed for anti-missiles—all in contradiction to the provisions of this Treaty. The U.S.S.R. also charges that the new PAVE PAW radar stations being deployed on the Atlantic and Pacific coasts and in the South provide radar-backing for an ABM Defense, and therefore is in violation of this Treaty. The Kremlin states that no measures have yet been taken to allay the U.S.S.R. concern. Also of asserted concern to the U.S.S.R. is President Reagan's endorsement in March 1983 of space-based ABM Systems which would clearly mean abrogation of the Treaty.

Sources:

"The President's Report to the Congress on Soviet Noncompliance with Arms Control Agreements," *The White House, Office of the Press Secretary*

"Background Paper on Compliance Issues," *The Arms Control Association*

"Arms Control and Disarmament Agreements," *U.S. Arms Control and Disarmament Agency*

Section IV

The security gained by the United States and its allies through past arms control agreements and the prospects for further restraints on nuclear weapons are being threatened.

As a result, the United States and the Soviet Union will face a double-barreled arms race where all of us will lose.

Gerard C. Smith
Chief SALT I Negotiator
Nixon Administration

In previous eras, great powers could continue to arm and consider themselves to be stronger and more secure. As the nuclear arms race developed, both the United States and the Soviet Union recognized that this simple principle no longer necessarily applied. The more each side armed with nuclear weapons, the less secure each might become.

An unlimited arms race—one without rules—might be so dangerous as to lead to the outbreak of a war which would have no victors.

Paul C. Warnke
Chief SALT II Negotiator
Carter Administration

The Effects of Nuclear War

The energy of a nuclear explosion is released in a number of different ways:

- an *explosive blast* which is qualitatively similar to the blast from ordinary chemical explosions but which has more devastating effects because it is typically so much larger;
- direct *nuclear radiation*;
- direct *thermal radiation*, most of which takes the form of visible light;
- pulses of electrical and magnetic energy called *electro-magnetic pulse* (EMP);
- the creation of a variety of radioactive particles which are thrown up into the air by the force of the blast and are called *radioactive fallout* when they return to Earth.

The distribution of the nuclear bomb's energy among these effects depends on its size and on the details of its design, but a general description is possible.

Blast

Most immediate damage to cities from large weapons comes from the explosive blast. The blast drives air away from the site of the explosion producing sudden changes in air pressure called "static overpressure" that can crush objects and destroy buildings. It also produces high winds called "dynamic pressure" that destroy people and objects such as trees and utility poles.

For the most part, blast kills people by indirect means. Most blast deaths result from the collapse of occupied buildings, from people being blown from buildings and into objects, or people being struck by flying objects.

Direct Nuclear Radiation

Nuclear weapons inflict ionizing radiation on people, animals, and plants in two different ways. **Direct radiation** occurs at the time of the explosion; it can be very intense, but its range is limited. **Fallout radiation** is received from particles that are made radioactive by the effects of the explosion and subsequently distributed at varying distances from the site of the blast.

For large nuclear weapons, the range of intense **direct radiation** is less than the range of **lethal blast** and **thermal radiation** effects. However, in the case of smaller weapons, "direct radiation" may be the lethal effect with the greatest range. Direct radiation did substantial damage to the residents of Hiroshima and Nagasaki.

Thermal Radiation

Approximately 35 percent of the energy from a nuclear explosion is an intense burst of **thermal radiation**, i.e., heat. The effects are roughly comparable to the effect of a 2-second flash from an enormous sunlamp. Since thermal radiation travels at the speed of light, the flash of light and heat precedes the blast wave by several seconds—just as lightning is seen before the thunder is heard.

The visible light will produce "flashblindness" in people who are looking in the direction of the explosion. This flashblindness would last for several minutes, after which recovery would be total. A one megaton explosion could cause flashblindness at distances as great as 13 miles on a clear day, or 53 miles on a clear night.

Skin burns result from higher intensities of light and therefore take place closer to the point of explosion. A one megaton explosion can cause

1st degree burns at distances of about 7 miles;

2nd degree burns at distances of about 6 miles, producing blisters that lead to infection if untreated and permanent scars;

3rd degree burns at distances of up to 5 miles, destroying skin tissue.

If 24 to 30 percent of the body is covered with second or third degree burns, this will result in serious shock and probably prove fatal unless prompt, specialized medical care is available. The entire United States has facilities to treat 1000 to 2000 severe burn cases—a single nuclear weapon could produce more than 10,000.

Fires

The **thermal radiation** from a nuclear explosion can directly ignite kindling materials. Fires most likely to spread are those caused by thermal radiation passing through windows, igniting beds and overstuffed furniture inside houses.

Another possible source of fires, which might be more damaging in urban areas, is indirect. **Blast damage** to stores, water heaters, furnaces, electrical circuits, or gas lines would ignite fires where fuel is plentiful.

It is possible that individual fires, whether caused by "thermal radiation" or by "blast damage" to utilities, furnaces, etc., would coalesce into a mass fire that would consume all structures over a large area. Mass fires could be of two kinds:

a **firestorm** in which violent inrushing winds create extremely high temperatures but prevent the fire from spreading radially outward such as the firestorms experienced in Hamburg, Tokyo, and Hiroshima in World War II; and

a **conflagration** in which a fire spreads along a front such as the Great Chicago fire and the San Francisco earthquake fire.

Electromagnetic Pulse (EMP)

Electromagnetic pulse is an **electromagnetic wave** similar to radio waves which results from secondary reactions occurring when the nuclear gamma radiation is absorbed in the air or ground. Most equipment designed to protect electrical facilities from lightning works too slowly to be effective against EMP.

There is no evidence that EMP is a physical threat to humans. However electrical or electronic systems, particularly those connected to long wires such as powerlines or antennas, can undergo physical damage such as a shorting of a capacitor or burnout of a transistor, and at a lesser level, a temporary operational upset.

Fallout

While any nuclear explosion in the atmosphere produces some fallout, the *fallout* is far greater if the burst is on the surface, or at least low enough for the fireball to touch the ground. Fallout from air bursts alone poses long-term health hazards, but they are trivial compared to the other consequences of a nuclear attack. The significant hazards come from particles scooped up from the ground and irradiated by the nuclear explosion.

The radioactive particles in the stem of the familiar mushroom cloud, that rise only a short distance, will fall back to earth within a matter of minutes, landing close to the center of the explosion. Such particles are unlikely to be the cause of many deaths because they will fall in areas where most people have already been killed. However, the radioactivity will complicate efforts at rescue or eventual reconstruction.

The radioactive particles that rise higher will be carried some distance by the wind before returning to Earth. Hence the area and intensity of the fallout is strongly influenced by local weather conditions. Much of the material is simply blown downwind in a long plume. "Wind direction" can make an enormous difference. "Rainfall" can also have a significant influence on the ways in which radiation from smaller weapons is deposited, since rain will carry contaminated particles to the ground. The areas receiving such contaminated rainfall would become **hot spots** with greater radiation intensity than their surroundings. When the radiation intensity from fallout is great enough to pose an immediate threat to health, fallout will generally be visible as a thin layer of dust.

Some radioactive particles will be thrust into the stratosphere and may not return to earth for some years. In this case only particularly long-lived particles pose a threat, and they would be dispersed around the world over a range of latitudes. Some fallout from U.S. and Soviet weapons tests in the 1950's and early 1960's can still be detected.

The biological effects of fallout radiation are substantially the same as those from direct radiation. People exposed to enough fallout radiation will die, and those exposed to lesser amounts may become ill.

The TTAPS Report – Nuclear Winter

In late 1983, a group of 40 distinguished scientists released a study, the TTAPS Report, on the global atmospheric and climatic effects that would be caused by a nuclear war.

Summarized, the four known principal consequences that would occur after a nuclear war are: obscuring smoke in the troposphere (7 to 10 miles from the Earth's surface); obscuring dust in the stratosphere (upper portion of the atmosphere); fallout of radioactive debris; and partial destruction of the ozone layer which shields and protects the Earth from the deadly ultraviolet radiation of the Sun.

Based on new findings concerning the Earth's thin ozone layer, the report concludes that the dust, especially the soot, would absorb ordinary visible light from the Sun, thus reducing the amount of sunlight penetrating the Earth's surface. The heavy toxic overcast would last for months and longer, making photosynthesis and thereby all plant growth impossible. Land temperatures would drop to 13 degrees below zero. Carl Sagan, the renowned scientist, predicts a **Nuclear Winter** where temperatures would drop so catastrophically that virtually all crops and farm animals would be destroyed as would most varieties of uncultivated or undomesticated food supplies. Most survivors of heat, blast, and radiation thus would starve.

This study has been endorsed by over 100 scientists and biologists including scientists from the Soviet Union.

Sources: "The Effects of Nuclear War," 79-60080
Office of Technology Assessment

"The Effects of Nuclear War,"
U.S. Arms Control and Disarmament Agency; Office of Operations Analysis

"Nuclear Winter: Global Consequences of Multiple Nuclear Explosions,"
The TTAPS Report; The Center on the Consequences of Nuclear War

Civil Defense

Civil defense seeks to protect the population, protect industry, and improve the quality of post-attack life, institutions, and values. The extent to which specific civil defense measures would succeed in doing so is controversial.

Some observers argue that U.S. civil defense promotes "deterrence" by increasing the credibility of U.S. retaliation and by reducing any Soviet destructive advantage in a nuclear war. Others, however, argue that preparations to survive a nuclear war in the United States and the Soviet Union will stimulate fears that increase the likelihood of nuclear war.

Since the Federal Civil Defense Act of 1950, the civil defense function has been repeatedly reorganized. In 1978, Congress approved the combination of civil defense and peacetime disaster functions into a single agency. The Federal Emergency Management Agency (FEMA) incorporates all previous responsibilities given to the Defense Civil Preparedness Agency (DCPA) in the Defense Department, the Federal Protection Agency (FPA) in the General Services Administration, and the Federal Disaster Assistance Administration (FDAA) in the Department of Housing and Urban Development.

The Federal Emergency Management Agency (FEMA), in a joint effort with state and local governments, has developed the following plans and capabilities to be put into operation in case of nuclear attack.

Civil Protection

The thrust of this FEMA program is to protect the U.S. population by relocating people from larger cities and other potential risk areas over a period of several days during an acute crisis, and providing them with fallout protection and support.

The plan for "crisis relocation" calls for the evacuation of 150 million Americans from about 400 "high-risk" areas to about 2000 presumably lower risk "host" areas, primarily small, rural towns at least 50 miles away. "High-risk" areas comprise regions around 63 important military installations, and 330 other military/industrial installations, and urban areas with populations of 50,000 or more. Because organizing and transporting people to relocation areas presents a staggering logistics problem, the effectiveness of crisis relocation will depend on the ability to complete high quality plans, as well as to develop operational systems and capabilities. Also crucial is the assumption of several days of warning time.

FEMA plans include two types of shelters in "high-risk" areas and in "host" areas.

Blast Shelters are structures designed to offer substantial protection against direct nuclear effects: blast, thermal radiation, ionizing radiation, and related effects such as fires. Each shelter will include stocks of food, water, necessary medical supplies, sanitary facilities, and equipment for controlling temperature, humidity, and "air-quality" standards. With many people enclosed in an air-tight shelter, temperatures, humidity, and carbon dioxide content increase, oxygen availability decreases, and fetid materials accumulate. Surface fires are also a threat because of extreme temperatures, carbon monoxide, and other noxious gases.

Fallout Shelters are buried or semi-buried structures shielded from radiation by using different materials such as steel, concrete, earth, water, and wood which reduce radiation intensity by differing amounts. The overall effectiveness of fallout shelters depends on having adequate time, information, and materials to build or improve an expedient shelter; having sufficient food, water, and other supplies to last until the outside fallout decays to a safe level; and entering the shelter promptly before absorbing so much radiation as to contaminate it.

Direction and Control

The system FEMA envisions to direct and control the population consists primarily of a sophisticated state and local governmental communications net which will serve 3000 protected command posts called Emergency Operating Centers (EOCs) for use by civil defense officials. All command posts will be supplied with fallout protection, emergency power generators, food, water, medical and sanitation supplies, and ventilation and radiological detection devices.

Attack Warning

Warning will be passed over the National Warning System to over 1200 federal, state, and local warning points which operate 24 hours a day. Once warning has reached local levels, it will be passed to the public by sirens or other means. Almost half of the U.S. population is in areas that could receive outdoor warning within 15 minutes of the national warning signal. Dissemination of warning to the public, however, is inadequate in many places. FEMA proposes to improve the coverage of the National Warning System.

Emergency Public Information

Fallout protection, emergency power generators, and remote units have been provided for radio stations in the Emergency Broadcast System to permit broadcast of emergency information under fallout conditions. Because one-third of the stations are in high-risk areas and could be destroyed by blast, a program has been initiated by FEMA to protect 180 stations from electromagnetic pulse (EMP). About one-third of the more than 5000 localities have reported development of civil defense programs to provide authoritative information and instruction to the public in emergencies.

Radiological Defense

To assist the officials of the Emergency Operating Centers in reporting local nuclear war damage to federal authorities, FEMA will provide specially trained radiation experts called Radiological Defense Officers. They will attempt to predict local fallout patterns and advise other EOCs and the sheltered population on local conditions. To aid postattack recovery operations, FEMA has begun producing and refurbishing millions of radiological instruments to be distributed prior to attack to law enforcement personnel, shelter managers, EOCs, and others. These instruments are designed to monitor accumulated radiation doses and radiation levels and decay rates in and outside of shelters. Effective radiological defense would require an estimated 2.4 million people to be trained as radiological monitors in a crisis.

Citizen Training

Crisis training via news media must now be relied on to educate citizens on hazards and survival actions. FEMA plans to restore simulated-emergency exercises for key local and state officials. Other civil defense training activities will include survival information to the public during a period of developing crisis, training in the area of shelter management, and accelerated training of radiological defense personnel.

Industrial Protection

Efforts to preserve critical economic assets and thereby accelerate postattack recovery include industrial defense measures to make buildings or machinery more resistant to blast pressure, fire, and debris; and protective facilities, semiburied structures and sandbagging to shelter costly and critical equipment. Some industries such as petroleum refineries and chemical plants may be impossible to protect. FEMA is making considerable use of studies regarding the feasibility of protecting factories with anti-ballistic missiles and using mobile oil refineries. However, the degree to which protection or recovery is possible is unknown.

Continuity of Government

FEMA's Federal Preparedness Program is designed primarily to protect the leadership and essential functions of the Executive Branch before, during and after a nuclear war. Its central element is Continuity of Goverment (CoG), a highly classified program involving scores of secret protected facilities equipped with a variety of advanced data processors, communication and other information systems to carry out detailed nuclear emergency procedures and contingency plans. Currently, the backbone of the program is FEMA's relocation center system which was constructed to support the two primary CoG missions: Presidential Succession and Continuity of Essential Executive Agencies. Federal Relocation Centers (FRCs) are fallout-protected, self-supporting facilities supplied with state-of-the-art computer and communication systems to perform a variety of mobilization functions. Approximately 100 relocation centers are scattered throughout five states in a 350-mile radius around Washington, D.C. known as the Federal Relocation Arc. Most of these facilities are connected by satellite, microwave and high-frequency radio communications, as well as underground cables, to transmit and receive information.

Sources: "FEMA Attack Environment Manual,"
"A Citizen's Handbook,"
Federal Emergency Management Agency
"Civil Defense and Effects of Nuclear War," IPO174C
The Library of Congress, Congressional Research Service

"The Effects of Nuclear War," 79-60080
Office of Technology Assessment
"The Defense Monitor," ISSN 0195-6450
The Center for Defense Information

Arms Control Terms

air-launched cruise missile—See cruise missile.

airborne warning and control system (AWACS)—A flying command post. AWACS has the capacity to identify hostile aircraft and to control friendly air forces in either offensive or defensive missions.

anti-ballistic missile (ABM) system—A system of missiles and radars capable of defending against a ballistic-missile attack by destroying incoming offensive missiles. The defensive missiles may be armed with either nuclear or non-nuclear warheads.

anti-submarine warfare (ASW)—The detection, identification, tracking, and destruction of hostile submarines. ASW can be either strategic (aimed at neutralizing an opponent's ballistic-missile submarines), or tactical (concerned with the pursuit and destruction of submarines in a local situation for missions such as convoy defense and aircraft carrier defense).

arms control—Any unilateral action or multilateral plan, arrangement, or process, resting upon explicit or implicit international agreement, which limits or regulates any aspect of the following: the production, numbers, type configuration, and performance characteristics of weapon systems (including related command and control, logistics support, and intelligence arrangements or mechanisms); and the numerical strength, organization, equipment, deployment or employment of the armed forces retained by the parties.

arms limitation—See arms control.

arms transfer—The sale or grant of arms from one nation to another.

ballistic missile—A missile, classified by range, that moves on a free-falling trajectory under the influence of gravity.

ballistic missile defense (BMD)—See ABM system.

binary nerve gas—A toxic gas created by the mixture of two relatively harmless chemicals during the final trajectory stage of a missile, bomb, or shell in which the gases are loaded. Because its two components are non-toxic until they are combined, binary gas can be stored and handled more easily than other toxic gases.

bomber—An aircraft, usually classified by range, capable of delivering nuclear and non-nuclear ordnance. Long-range bombers are those capable of traveling 6000 or more miles on one load of fuel; medium-range bombers can travel between 3500 and 6000 miles without refueling.

breeder reactor—A reactor that produces more nuclear fuel than it consumes while generating power.

circular error probable (CEP)—A measure of missile accuracy. It is the radius of a circle around a target in which 50 percent of the missiles aimed at that target will land.

civil defense—All those activities and measures designed to minimize the effects upon the civilian population caused by an enemy attack upon the United States; to deal with immediate emergency conditions and to effectuate emergency restoration of vital utilities and facilities destroyed by such attack.

command, control, communication, and intelligence (C^3I)—The "nerves" of military operations, that is, information-processing systems used to detect, assess, and respond to actual and potential military and political crisis situations or conflicts. C^3I includes systems which manage materiel and manpower during crises or conflicts, as well as in peacetime.

confidence-building measures—Measures taken to demonstrate a nation's lack of belligerent or hostile *intent*, as distinguished from measures which actually reduce military *capabilities*. Confidence-building measures can be negotiated or unilateral. The division between confidence-building measures and arms control measures is not strict; the former may involve, for example, troop withdrawals, while the latter may aim more at securing trust than limiting weaponry.

counterforce—Directed against an opponent's military forces and military industry. Used to describe military strategies, attacks, weapons, etc.

countervalue—Directed against an opponent's civilian and economic centers. Used to describe military strategies, attacks, weapons, etc.

crisis stability—A strategic situation in which neither side has an incentive to use nuclear weapons during a crisis.

cruise missile—A pilotless missile, propelled by an air-breathing jet engine, that flies in the atmosphere. Cruise missiles may be armed with either conventional or nuclear warheads and launched from an aircraft, a submarine or surface ship, or land-based platform.

damage limitation—The capacity to reduce damage from a nuclear attack by passive or active defenses or by striking the opponent's forces in a counterforce attack.

dense pack—A basing proposal for the MX missile in which silos are placed very close together. Supporters of the dense pack system argue that incoming missile "fratricide" will increase MX survivability.

deterrence—Dissuasion of a potential adversary from initiating an attack or conflict, often by the threat of unacceptable retaliatory damage. Nuclear deterrence is usually contrasted with the concept of nuclear defense, the strategy and forces for limiting damage, if deterrence fails. Some hold that a strategy of nuclear defense may also have a deterrent effect, if it can reduce the destructive potential of a nuclear attack.

disarmament—In UN usage, all measures related to the prevention, limitation, reduction, or elimination of weapons and military forces. See general and complete disarmament.

fallout The spread of radioactive particles from clouds of debris produced by nuclear blasts. "Local fallout" falls to the Earth's surface within twenty-four hours of the blast.

first strike—An initial attack with nuclear weapons. A *disarming* first strike is one in which the attacker attempts to destroy all or a large portion of its adversary's strategic nuclear forces before they can be launched. A *preemptive* first strike is one in which a nation launches its attack first on the presumption that the adversary is about to attack.

first use—The introduction of nuclear weapons into a strategic or tactical conflict. See first strike. A no-first-use pledge by a nation obliges it not to be the first to introduce nuclear weapons in a conflict.

fission—The process of splitting atomic nuclei through bombardment of neutrons. This process yields vast quantities of energy as well as more neutrons capable of initiating further fission.

fratricide—The destruction or degradation of the accuracy and effectiveness of an attacking nuclear weapon by the nearby explosion of another attacking nuclear weapon.

fractionation—The division of bomber or missile payload into separate re-entry vehicles.

freeze—See nuclear freeze.

fusion—The process of combining atomic nuclei to form a single heavier element or nucleus and to release large amounts of energy.

general and complete disarmament (GCD)—The total abandonment of military forces and weapons (other than internal police forces) by all nations at the same time, usually foreseen as occurring through an agreed schedule of force reductions. In 1961, in the so-called McCloy-Zorin Principles, the United States and the U.S.S.R. agreed that their negotiations would have GCD as their ultimate objective.

ground-launched cruise missile (GLCM)—See cruise missile.

hard or hardened target—A target protected against the blast, heat, and radiation effects of nuclear weapons of specific yields. Hardening is usually accomplished by means of earth and reinforced concrete and is measured by the number of pounds per square inch of blast overpressure which a target can withstand.

intercontinental ballistic missile (ICBM)—A ballistic missile with a range of 4000 or more nautical miles. Conventionally, the term ICBM is used only for land-based systems, to differentiate them from submarine-launched ballistic missiles, which also have an intercontinental range.

intermediate nuclear forces (INF)—A term coined by U.S. officials to emphasize the links between U.S. strategic weapons and theater weapons in Europe. In its original meaning, it was synonymous with long-range theater nuclear forces (LRTNF). More recently, it has been expanded to include all TNF except battlefield weapons. Negotiations between the U.S. and the U.S.S.R., opened in November 1981, seek to limit the European-based, intermediate-range nuclear forces of both sides. (See also theater nuclear forces, long-range theater nuclear forces).

kiloton—A measure of the yield of a nuclear weapon, equivalent to 1000 tons of TNT.

launch-on-warning doctrine—A strategic doctrine under which a nation's bombers and land-based missiles would be launched on receipt of warning (from satellites and other early-warning systems) that an opponent had launched its missiles. This doctrine is sometimes also called "launch on positive (or confirmed) notification of attack" to distinguish between possible and actual attack. Sometimes recommended for use when there is uncertainty over the ability of fixed-site strategic weapons (e.g., ICBMs) to survive an attack, a launch-on-warning doctrine is viewed as destabilizing in a crisis situation.

light-water reactor—The most common type of nuclear power reactor. It is fueled by enriched uranium. The spent fuel of a light-water reactor contains significant amounts of plutonium which could be used to make nuclear explosives.

Mark 12A warhead—A new warhead for the Minuteman III missile. The increased accuracy and yield of the Mark 12A re-entry vehicles in the warhead will increase the ability of the Minuteman III missiles to destroy hardened Soviet missile silos and other targets.

megaton—A measure of the yield of a nuclear weapon, equivalent of 1,000,000 tons of TNT.

missile experimental (MX)—A U.S. ICBM which is designed to replace the current ICBM force during the 1980s. This more accurate, powerful, and destructive missile could be deployed in either a single silo or mobile mode and would be capable of destroying Soviet missile silos.

multiple independently-targetable re-entry vehicle (MIRV)—A package of two or more re-entry vehicles which can be carried by a single ballistic missile and delivered on separate targets. The term MIRV is also commonly used for a missile with a MIRVed warhead or for the process of switching from single to multiple re-entry vehicles.

mutual assured destruction—A concept of reciprocal deterrence which rests on the ability of the two nuclear superpowers to inflict unacceptable damage on one another after surviving a nuclear first strike.

national technical means (NTM)—A method of verifying compliance with negotiated arms control agreements generally consistent with the recognized provisions of international law, commonly understood as surveillance by satellite and aerial reconnaissance.

neutron bomb—A tactical nuclear warhead designed to enhance radiation effects. It would be carried on artillery shells and short-range missiles, primarily for defense against a tank and heavy armored attack by the Warsaw Pact. The purported advantage is minimization of blast damage in friendly territory.

no-first-use doctrine—A no-first-use pledge by a nation obliges it not to introduce nuclear weapons first into a conflict. (See first use.)

nuclear freeze—The generic term for a variety of proposals calling for a halt to the testing, production, and deployment of all nuclear weapons and delivery systems. Proposals have been introduced in both houses of Congress, numerous local and town councils, and a variety of state legislatures.

nuclear fuel cycle—Any process for developing, utilizing, and disposing of nuclear fuels.

nuclear weapon-free zone—An area in which the production and deployment of nuclear weapons is prohibited.

on-site inspection—A method of verifying compliance with an arms control agreement whereby representatives of an international or other designated organization, or of the parties to the agreement, are given direct access to view force deployments or weapon systems.

parity—A level of forces in which opposing nations possess approximately equal capabilities.

peaceful nuclear explosion (PNE)—The non-military use of nuclear detonations for such purposes as stimulating natural gas, recovering oil shale, diverting rivers, or excavating.

Pershing II—Deployment began in 1983. The Pershing II is the successor system to the Pershing IA IRBM. The Pershing II incorporates the new RADAG guidance system, making it an extremely accurate and mobile weapon.

plutonium—An element not found in nature which is created as a waste product of nuclear reactors. Plutonium can be used to make nuclear weapons.

pounds per square inch (psi)—A measure of nuclear blast overpressure or dynamic pressure used to calculate the effects of a nuclear detonation or the ability of a structure to withstand a nuclear blast.

preemptive strike—A damage-limiting attack launched in anticipation of an opponent's attack.

proliferation—The spread of weapons, usually nuclear weapons. Horizontal proliferation refers to the acquisition of nuclear weapons by states not previously possessing them. Vertical proliferation refers to increases in the nuclear arsenals of those states already possessing nuclear weapons.

re-entry vehicle—That part of a ballistic missile designed to re-enter the Earth's atmosphere in the terminal portion of its trajectory.

reprocessing plant—A facility required to separate the uranium and plutonium present in spent reactor fuel. The plutonium recovered through reprocessing can be reused as reactor fuel or for nuclear explosives.

sea-launched cruise missile (SLCM)—See cruise missile.

second strike—A follow-up or retaliatory attack after an opponent's first strike. Second-strike capability describes the capacity to attack after suffering a first strike. The U.S. strategy of deterrence is premised on high confidence in the ability of the United States to deliver a nuclear second strike that would inflict unacceptable damage on the nation which struck first.

Standing Consultative Commission (SCC)—A joint U.S.-U.S.S.R. negotiating body, established by the ABM Treaty, which meets semi-annually to review implementation of the ABM Treaty and other strategic arms limitation agreements in force.

strategic—Relating to a nation's offensive or defensive military potential, including its geographical location and its resources and economic, political, and military strength. The term strategic is used to denote those weapons or forces capable of directly affecting another nation's war-fighting ability, as distinguished from tactical or theater weapons or forces.

Strategic Arms Limitation Talks (SALT)—Negotiations between the United States and the U.S.S.R. initiated in 1969 which seek to limit the strategic nuclear forces, both offensive and defensive, of both sides.

Strategic Arms Reduction Talks (START)—Negotiations between the U.S./U.S.S.R., formerly named SALT, which were started in June 1982 to seek reductions in the strategic arsenals of both sides. The change in name came as a result of the Reagan Administration's desire to emphasize reductions rather than mere limitations in nuclear weapons.

Strategic Talks on Prevention of Nuclear War (STOP)—An arms control negotiating position which focuses specifically on measures to achieve stability and prevent the use of nuclear weapons.

submarine-launched ballistic missile (SLBM)—Any ballistic missile launched from a submarine.

tactical—Relating to battlefield operations as distinguished from theater or strategic operations. Tactical weapons or forces are those designed for combat with opposing military forces rather than for reaching the rear areas of the opponent or the opponent's homeland, which require theater or strategic weapons, respectively.

telemetry—The transmission of electronic signals by missiles to Earth. Monitoring these signals aids in evaluating a weapon's performance and provides a way of verifying weapon tests undertaken by an adversary.

theater nuclear weapon (TNW)—A nuclear weapon, usually of longer range and larger yield than a tactical nuclear weapon, which can be used in theater operations. Many strategic nuclear weapons can be used in theater operations, but not all theater nuclear weapons are designed for strategic use. The Soviet SS-20 mobile missile is generally considered a theater nuclear weapon, as are the nuclear-capable U.S. fighter/bombers deployed in the Far East and Europe and the U.S. Lance missile.

throw-weight—The maximum weight of the warheads, guidance unit, and penetration aids which can be delivered by a missile over a particular range and in a stated trajectory.

triad—U.S. strategic forces which are composed of three parts: land-based intercontinental ballistic missiles; submarine-launched ballistic missiles; and long-range bombers.

uranium—A heavy silvery-white metallic element, radioactive, easily oxidized, and having 14 known isotopes of which U238 is the most abundant in nature.

vertical short take-off and landing (V/STOL)—Relating to the ability of an aircraft vertically to clear a 50-foot obstacle within 1500 feet after takeoff or stop within 1500 feet over a 50-foot obstacle in landing. An advantage of V/STOL aircraft is that they are able to operate nearer the forward edge of the battle area.

warhead—That part of a missile, torpedo, rocket, or other munition which contains either the nuclear or thermonuclear system, chemical or biological agent, or inert materials intended to inflict damage.

yield—The force of a nuclear explosion expressed as the equivalent of the energy produced by tons of TNT. See kiloton and megaton.

Sources: "SALT II Agreement," Selected Documents No. 12A
U.S. Department of State

"A Glossary of Arms Control Terms,"
The Arms Control Association

Acronyms Used in Nuclear Weapons Issues

ABM	Anti-Ballistic Missile
ALBM	Air-Launched Ballistic Missile
ALCM	Air-Launched Cruise Missile
ASBM	Air-to-Surface Ballistic Missile
ASW	Anti-Submarine Warfare
AWACS	Airborne Warning and Control System
BMD	Ballistic Missile Defense
CCD	Conference of the Committee on Disarmament
CD	Committee on Disarmament
CEP	Circular Error Probable
C³I	Command, Control, Communications, and Intelligence
CM	Cruise Missile
CSCE	Conference on Security and Cooperation in Europe
CTBT	Comprehensive Test Ban Treaty
DOD	Department of Defense
FBS	Forward-Based System
GLCM	Ground-Launched Cruise Missile
HB	Heavy Bomber
ICBM	InterContinental Ballistic Missile
INF	Intermediate Nuclear Forces
IRBM	Intermediate-Range Ballistic Missile
KT	Kiloton—1000 Tons of TNT
LRTNF	Long-Range Theater Nuclear Force
MBFR	Mutual and Balanced Force Reductions Talks
MIRV	Multiple Independently-Targetable Re-entry Vehicle
MRBM	Medium-Range Ballistic Missile
MT	Megaton—1,000,000 Tons of TNT
MX	Missile eXperimental
NPT	NonProliferation Treaty
NTM	National Technical Means
PSI	Pounds Per Square Inch
R&D	Research and Development
RV	Reentry Vehicle
SALT	Strategic Arms Limitation Talks
SAM	Surface-to-Air Missile
SCC	Standing Consultative Commission
SLBM	Submarine-Launched Ballistic Missile
SLCM	Sea-Launched Cruise Missile
SRAM	Short-Range Attack Missile
SRBM	Short-Range Ballistic Missile
SSBN	Nuclear-Propelled Ballistic-Missile-Bearing Submarine
START	Strategic Arms Reduction Talks
STOP	Strategic Talks on Prevention of Nuclear War
TTBT	Threshold Test Ban Treaty

Source: The majority of acronyms compiled from:
"A Glossary of Arms Control Terms,"
The Arms Control Association

Index